**W9-BDC-934**

ARE YOU ENOUGH OF A HOOP FAN TO ANSWER THESE QUIZZES WITHOUT GETTING TRADED?

1) Who is the Hawk who has led his team in scoring in each of the past seven years?

2) Who was the Knick who finished fourth in assists and second in steals in 1979–80?

3) The fabulous players from the 1948–49 Kentucky Wildcats became player-owners of what pro team in 1949–50?

4) The Minneapolis-Los Angeles Lakers have had twelve head coaches. Who was the coach from 1960 to 1967?

1) John Drew
2) Michael Ray Richardson
3) Indianapolis Olympians
4) Fred Schaus

Quintessential Quiz Books from SIGNET

(0451)

☐ THE ELVIS PRESLEY TRIVIA QUIZ BOOK by Helen Rosenbaum. (081781—$1.50)

☐ THE SOAP OPERA TRIVIA QUIZ BOOK by Jason Bonderoff. (117506—$2.75)*

☐ THE ROLLING STONES TRIVIA QUIZ BOOK by Helen Rosenbaum. (086694—$1.75)

☐ THE SUPERHERO MOVIE AND TV TRIVIA QUIZ BOOK by Jeff Rovin. (084748—$1.75)*

☐ THE OFFICIAL TV TRIVIA QUIZ BOOK #2 by Bart Andrews. (084101—$1.50)

☐ THE NOSTALGIA QUIZ BOOK by Martin A. Gross. (110358—$2.50)*

☐ THE OFFICIAL ROCK 'N' ROLL TRIVIA QUIZ BOOK #2 by Marc Sotkin. (084853—$1.50)

☐ TREKKIE QUIZ BOOK by Bart Andrews. (084136—$1.50)

☐ THE SUPER SIXTIES QUIZ BOOK by Bart Andrews. (088298—$1.75)*

☐ FROM THE BLOB TO STAR WARS by Bart Andrews. (079485—$1.50)

☐ THE FIRST OFFICIAL NFL TRIVIA QUIZ BOOK by Ted Brock and Jim Campbell. (095413—$1.95)

☐ THE SECOND NFL TRIVIA QUIZ BOOK by Jim Campbell. (117891—$2.25)*

☐ THE ULTIMATE BASEBALL QUIZ BOOK by Dom Forker. (096797—$2.50)*

☐ THE ULTIMATE YANKEE BASEBALL QUIZ BOOK by Dom Forker. (114299—$2.95)*

☐ THE ULTIMATE WORLD SERIES QUIZ BOOK by Dom Forker. (117883—$1.95)*

*Price slightly higher in Canada

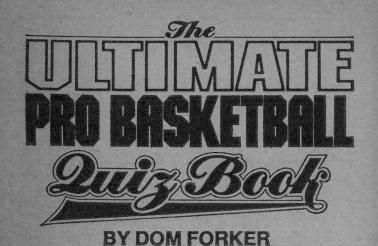

The ULTIMATE PRO BASKETBALL Quiz Book

BY DOM FORKER

A SIGNET BOOK
NEW AMERICAN LIBRARY
TIMES MIRROR

To Tim, the oldest of my three sports-loving sons, and the first of them to help me with my research

Acknowledgments

The author is appreciative of the fact that he had solid sources for his research. He would like to credit and congratulate those people who were responsible for the publication of the following books:

Champions

Complete Handbook of Pro Basketball

NBA Guide

NBA Register

NBA's Official Encyclopedia of Pro Basketball

Pro Digest

In addition, he would like to credit and congratulate his oldest son, Tim, for the valuable assistance he gave his dad in the research and creation of this book. Tim was a constant reminder of another 18-year-old boy, many years ago at the 69th Regiment Armory, begging Dick McGuire to "Shoot, Dick, shoot!"

Finally, I value the conversations about pro basketball that I've had with Dick Dzury, a teaching colleague and friend of mine, and undoubtedly the *ultimate* number-one fan of the Boston Celtics.

Contents

Introduction   1

The First Quarter   7

The Second Quarter   47

The Third Quarter   109

The Fourth Quarter   146

Answers   187

Introduction

When I was a teenager, in the early-to-mid 1950s, I rooted for the New York Knickerbockers. They did not have a great deal of height. But they were fast and they played team ball.

In the back court they had Dick McGuire and Carl Braun. "Tricky Dick," we used to call McGuire. He was a masterful playmaker. I can remember many nights at the 69th Regiment Armory when the defense would slough off him and the fans would plead with him, "Shoot, Dick, shoot!" Sooner or later, Dick would take his set shot from downtown; and, more times than not, he would swish the nets. But he got much more satisfaction out of setting up a picture-perfect play than he did of hitting his eight-point-a-game career average. And so did we.

Carl Braun, at the other guard, could pop from outside with the best of the shooting guards. He would spring off the floor like an Olympic diver lifting effortlessly off the board, and he would follow through with perfect symmetry. One night, at the age of 19, he scored a record 47 points in one game.

Harry Gallatin and Sweetwater Clifton, two well-built forwards, manned the corners, hit the boards hard, and shot effectively from short range. Clifton was a trailblazer in the art of the slam dunk, which was the main topic of discussion during the pregame warmups. In the pivot was Connie Simmons, a castoff from the 1947–48 champion Baltimore Bullets, who used to complement McGuire beautifully on the give-and-go.

Vince Boryla could play the corner and the pivot, too. And he was a deadly foul shooter. I can still see him standing at the foul line, bouncing the ball five, six times before he deliberately and methodically would swish the net.

In reserve was Ernie Vandeweghe, the first "true" sixth man. The "Doctor" used to come off the bench and prescribe the fast break that would give the Knicks the momentum they needed. He also had a fetish about taking the last shot in the pregame and the halftime warmups.

Joe Lapchick, the coach, added an extra element of class to the club. He was a throwback to the Original Celtics, and he was a successful NIT-winning coach at St. John's University before and after his nine years with the Knicks.

Even the announcer of the Knicks' games stands out in memory. Was there ever another announcer who could describe play-by-play like Marty Glickman? He was "Good . . . like Nedick's!" He wove a tapestry of beautiful imagery that captivated our fanciful imaginations.

Then one day the game changed. Dick McGuire chronicled the change when he said, "The game's not the same anymore. We used to come up court, set up a pattern, and execute it for a basket in twenty to twenty-five seconds. Now the other team comes right back and neutralizes that basket in five seconds. Things have changed."

"Things" continue to change. Today if you don't have a field-goal shooting percentage of .500, you are considered suspect as a shooter. Does that mean that Jerry West, who shot .500 or better in only one of his 14 professional seasons, would be a marginal player today? I leave it to you to decide.

From my point of view, I like quick "little" men who play team basketball. That's why, I suppose, I relate to another New York team, the 1969–70 Knickerbockers.

Knick fans had waited faithfully, but forlornly, for 25 years, hoping and praying for the championship that always managed to elude them, comparing present-day players to the McGuires and the Brauns as the yardstick of Knick greatness, when suddenly the team they were watching became the team they remembered. Only *better!*

Walt Frazier was "Clyde," gliding gracefully in and out of traffic, dribbling the 24-second clock away and hitting

2

his turnaround jumper at the buzzer. Dick Barnett, also in the back court, complemented Frazier in every possible way that the off-guard can: steals, assists, and baskets.

Bill Bradley, the weak-side forward, had the knack of moving without the ball, getting open, and hitting the big basket. Why not? He was "Dollar Bill." Dave DeBusschere, the strong-side forward, could blister the nets. He could also bang the boards, hit the open man, and play defense. In fact, he made the All-NBA First-Team Defense in each of his last six years in the league. He was, in short, "Big D."

In the middle there was—well, that's what the history of this game is all about. There was Willis Reed, 6-10 and 240 pounds, a five-year player out of Grambling College.

It's no wonder that Knick fans feel special about Willis, for Willis did something special for them in 1969–70. After 25 years of agonized waiting and hoping, they were elevated one night—on the evening of the seventh game of the 1969–70 championship series—by the courage and grit of Number 19, who inspired his teammates to reach for greatness and leave their mark on the history of the NBA.

Coming off a regular-season scoring average of 21.7 points a game, Willis was the recipient of the MVP Award. In the playoffs he was his usual solid self until the fifth game, with the series tied at two games apiece, when he tore muscles in his thigh. The Knicks in that game miraculously came back from a 16-point deficit to win; but in the sixth game, played in Los Angeles, the Lakers, encouraged by the absence of Willis, romped to a 135–113 win behind Wilt Chamberlain's 45 points.

The Knicks, returning to New York for Game Seven, were tied in games but down in heart. There seemed to be little chance of their winning without the presence of Willis. And that's exactly what it took—his presence. At 7:34 p.m., exactly one minute before the game was scheduled to start, Willis, strengthened slightly by an injection in his thigh, emerged from the runway that leads from the dressing room and hobbled on to the floor. It was truly one of the great moments of sport. The overflow crowd rose as

3

one man to applaud the big man's courage. Literally every pair of eyes at Madison Square Garden, including those of the Los Angeles Lakers, focused on the big man as he labored with a couple of practice shots. The Lakers saw two things: one, a counterfeit copy of the player who had been so unstoppable until his injury in Game Five and, two, a presentiment of things to come.

Willis sank only two baskets in that game. But they were the first two, and they turned out to be the only two that the Knicks would need from Willis. He gave them the momentum they needed to break to a 113–99 win and the club's first NBA championship.

Some observers said that Reed's presence gave the Knicks the confidence they needed. Other witnesses said that his presence took away the Lakers' confidence. Both viewpoints are probably correct. What is undoubtedly correct is that Reed's appearance was one of the most dramatic moments in the history of sports.

Though he was not an offensive threat that night, he did stand out on defense. Hobbled as he was, he neutralized Chamberlain defensively until he left the game in the third quarter. "The Big Dipper," who had scored 45 points in Game Six, tallied only 13 points in the championship game.

The 1969–70 team is now the yardstick of Knick greatness. It was not big as big teams go, it was not fast as fast teams go, and it was not talented as talented teams go. But it was complete as complete teams go. And it was *my* team.

On that momentous night another Knick, often overlooked because of the symbolic significance of Reed's presence that evening, attained greatness, too. With the pressure on the line, he rose to the occasion by scoring 36 points and handing off a playoff record 19 assists.

Who is that sometimes forgotten hero?

Answer: Walt Frazier

The Playing Rules

The playing rules of The *Ultimate Pro Basketball Quiz Book* are simple. You just have to outscore your opponent who, in this case, happens to be the book itself. But the book represents the history of pro basketball, so the challenge is a formidable one.

The subject matter of "The First Quarter" is the NBA today; "The Second Quarter," the history of the game, its players and its teams; "The Third Quarter," the records of the NBA, the ABA, and the All Stars; and "The Fourth Quarter," baseline-to-baseline, every conceivable dimension of the game.

The most points ever scored in a game by one team were the 173 markers that were netted by the Boston Celtics against the Minneapolis Lakers in 1959. The most points scored by two teams in one game were the 316 markers run up by the Warriors (169) and the Knicks (147) in 1962.

Both of those records will fall during this court contest. The winner of this game will be the "team" that answers most of the questions. You have a chance to become the first "team" to score over 1,000 . . . 2,000 . . . 3,000 (?) points in a pro basketball "game."

There are 164 quizzes (games) in this book. That's twice as many games as the NBA teams play in a season. See how many quizzes (games) you can win. Place that number over the total number of games. Divide the top number by the bottom number, and compute the overall winning percentage. Compare that winning percentage mark with the top winning percentage marks under "Scoreboard" at the end of the book, and you will know how you stack up with the best teams that have ever played the game.

Occasionally there will be overlapping or repeat questions. That's not unusual in a 164-game schedule. Sooner or later, the same play is going to come your way. The important thing is, can you make that play?

Jump ball.

THE
FIRST
QUARTER

1. TODAY IN THE NBA

The references in this quiz are complete through the 1980–81 season.

1) _____ Who is the Hawk who has led his team in scoring in each of the past seven years?

2) _____ Who is the starter for the Hawks who recorded only 79 assists in 2,075 minutes of playing time during the 1980–81 season?

3) _____ Who is the Hawk forward who has led Atlanta in blocked shots and rebounds the past three years?

4) _____ Who is the cousin of Wayne Rollins who had his best year in assists, steals, and scoring (19.1) in 1980–81?

5) _____ Who is the smallest player in the NBA?

6) _____ Who is the present-day player who was a Rhodes scholar?

7) _____ Who is the former player who has been the only other player in NBA history to be a Rhodes scholar?

8) _____ Whose arrival in the NBA is credited with converting his team's victory output from 29 (the preceding year) to 61?

9) _____ Who is the East Coast big man who blocked 214 shots in 1980–81 after snuffing only 115 shots for a West Coast team the previous year?

10) _____ Who is the East Coast power forward who made 58.7 percent of his shots in his first four years in the pros?

11) _____ Who is the Celtic forward who is second to Mychal Thompson on Minnesota University's all-time scoring and rebounding lists?

12) _____ Who is the Celtic who led his team in free throws attempted and made from 1978–79 to 1980–81?

13) _____ Who is the East Coast floorman who won the scoring and assist titles in 1972–73, the only time the feat's ever been accomplished?

14) _____ Who is the 6-11, 230-pound center who played on a state champion in high school, an NCAA champion in college, and an NBA champion in the pros?

15) _____ Who is the Celtic standout who netted 70 of his three-point attempts in 1979–80?

16) _____ Who is the Celtic front-courtman who was originally drafted by the Celtics but chose St. Louis of the ABA instead?

17) _____ Who is the NBA's all-time field goal percentage leader?

18) _____ Who in 1980–81 was the only player to lead his team in scoring, assists, and steals?

19) _____ Who is the Bull who has not missed one game during his four-year career?

20) _____ Who is the UCLA product who was picked second, behind Magic Johnson, in the 1979 player draft?

21) _____ Who set an NBA record with 11 steals in one game?

22) _____ Who was the Cavaliers' 24.5 scorer in 1980–81 who also is the all-time leading scorer and rebounder at Auburn?

23) _____ Who is the power forward who averaged 15.9 points a game as a rookie for the 1976 ABA-winning New York Nets?

24) _____ Who is the Cavalier, a high school team-

mate of Adrian Dantley, who in 1980–81 averaged 15.2 points per game and finished sixth in the league in rebounds?

25) _____ Who is the Cavalier guard who went to Bradley on a baseball scholarship—he was offered a try-out by Cincinnati—and ended up breaking seven scoring records while averaging better than 27 points a game during his last two years?

26) _____ Who is the Cleveland playmaker who handed off 28 assists—one short of the record—in a 1981–82 game?

27) _____ Who is the Cavalier, a third-round draft choice, who played a year in Italy before joining the club?

28) _____ Who is Cleveland's "Mr. Consistency," a player who's averaged 15.2 to 16.7 points a game in his first four seasons?

29) _____ Who is the nifty back-courtman who scored more than 9,000 points in eight seasons—two of them abbreviated by injuries—with San Antonio?

30) _____ Who is the Maverick cornerman whose .887 free throw percentage was the best in the NBA among nonguards in 1980–81?

31) _____ Who is the Maverick forward who was a three-time Academic-All-America at North Carolina?

32) _____ Who is the former back-court teammate of John Lucas at Maryland who averaged nine assists a game in the games he started for Dallas in 1980–81?

33) _____ Who is the seven-year veteran of the pros who didn't play high school basketball because he was an outstanding trumpet player?

34) Who is the former Gary Cole? He changed his name.

35) _____ Who once scored 73 points in a pro game?

36) _____ Who is the former standout at Kentucky University who in 1980–81 became the twelfth player to score 20,000 points?

37) _____ Who is the back-courtman who was twice named College Player of the Year at North Carolina?

38) _____ Who is the Nuggets' rugged rebounder whose scoring stats have improved in each of his first five

years in the pros, leading to his being named to the 1981–82 All Star team?

39) _____ Who sank a record 78 consecutive free throws?

40) _____ Who is the player whose initials stand for Theodore Roosevelt?

41) _____ Who is the eight-year back-courtman who took a three-year break to train for a law career before resuming his three-point threat with the Nuggets in 1979–80?

42) _____ Who is the Piston distance shooter who broke Dave DeBusschere's scoring record at the University of Detroit?

43) _____ Who is the Piston who switched from center to forward midway through the 1980–81 season and turned in the best scoring effort (15.7) of his career?

44) _____ Who is the Piston who in 1980–81 led all forwards in blocked shots for the third consecutive year?

45) _____ Who is the seven-footer who once committed six personal fouls in one quarter?

46) _____ Who is the 6-3 guard—he's the second all-time leading scorer, behind Kareem Abdul-Jabbar, in the Pac-10—who was drafted by the San Diego Chargers even though he didn't play football in high school or college?

47) _____ Who is the 6-3 guard who came into his own after a trade to San Diego? He averaged 28.8, 30.2, and 24.1 points a game in his first three years with the Clippers.

48) _____ Who was the latter part of the "Ernie and Bernie Show" at Tennessee?

49) _____ Who was the former part?

50) _____ Who is the Warrior guard who took 198 shots in 1980–81, 116 of which were three-point attempts? He made 53 from long range.

51) _____ Who is the 6-4 guard who has recorded most of his 3,000-or-so assists feeding Artis Gilmore in Kentucky, Julius Erving in New York, and George Gervin in San Antonio?

52) _____ Who is the 6-3 guard for Washington who

once (in 1977) tied an NBA record with 12 assists in one quarter?

53) _____ Who is the one-time scoring champ who came into the NBA directly from high school?

54) _____ Who is the 25,000-point scorer who missed only seven games in his first 13 years in the pros?

55) _____ Who is the 5-9 guard who has averaged 20 points a game five times?

56) _____ Who is the Houston forward who had two 27-point games against the Celtics in the 1980–81 championship series?

57) _____ Who is the reserve guard for Houston who started for two Washington teams, including the championship club of 1977–78?

58) _____ Who is the lesser-known Jones brother who twice (1975 and 1976) led NCAA Division II in rebounding?

59) _____ Who is the Knick shot-blocker who is known as "The Human Eraser?"

60) _____ Who is the Pacer 10,000-point scorer who once strung together points-per-game seasons of 28.1, 26.6, and 22.9?

61) _____ Who was the Jack McKinney product at St. Joe's (Pa.) who also played for his college mentor in the pros at Indiana?

62) _____ Who was the Indiana forward who missed six games in 1980–81 after running into a Darryl Dawkins elbow, then took "Dr. Dunk's" place in the 76er starting five when the backboard breaker "broke" his leg in 1981–82?

63) _____ Who is the 21.7 points-per-game career scorer who was the scapegoat of the 76ers' championship-game loss to Portland in 1976–77?

64) _____ Who is the Pacer who was the front part of the "Louie and Bouie (Roosevelt) Show" at Syracuse?

65) _____ Who is the Pacer who once averaged 29.8 points a game in one season?

66) _____ Who is the well-traveled player (six ABA teams and three NBA clubs) who was one of the two cen-

ters on the Baltimore Claws, the ABA team which never played a game?

67) _____ Who is another present-day player who was the other center of the Claws?

68) _____ Who is the present-day Pacer who has sunk 189 three-pointers in his career and once made the All-Defensive Team four straight years?

69) _____ Who is the King point guard who averaged 16.5 points a game and eight assists per contest in the first three years of his pro career?

70) _____ Who is the King forward who scored just under 20 points a game as a 20-year-old Net in 1980–81?

71) _____ Who is the center, perhaps the best passing pivotman, who scored his 10,000th point while a member of the Nets in 1981–82?

72) _____ Who is the naturalized Romanian citizen who became the first collegian to play for the United States in Israel's Maccabean Games?

73) _____ Who is the big man for the Kings who, despite a .573 shooting percentage in 1980–81, scored only six points a game?

74) _____ Who is the 6-10 King who played guard in the final game of Kansas City's playoff series with Phoenix in 1980–81?

75) _____ Who is the Kansas City guard who set a playoff record in 1978 when he handed off eight assists in one quarter?

76) _____ Who is the second leading scorer in the history of the game?

77) _____ Who has four times averaged 30 points a game?

78) _____ Who led a college team to an NCAA championship at the age of 19 and a pro team to an NBA title at the age of 20?

79) _____ Who is the Laker back-courtman who has played next to 13 other guards during his five-year career in Los Angeles?

80) _____ Who is the Laker forward who averaged 20 points a game in 1979–80 and 22.6 points a game in 1980–81?

12

81) _____ Who is the larcenous guard from Rutgers who is known as "The Thief of Baghdad?"

82) _____ Who was the sixth-man forward with Washington who has won a starting job with the Lakers?

83) _____ Who is the Milwaukee Buck—he has a 20-point career average—who was named College Player of the Year in 1977?

84) _____ Who is the Buck who has his size "22" sneakers displayed at the Hall of Fame? His 20-point-plus average over 14 seasons may get his body into those sneakers someday.

85) _____ Who in 1980–81 led all sixth men in scoring for the third straight year?

86) _____ Who is the Buck who guided Indiana to an undefeated season and NCAA title and captained the Olympic team to a gold medal in 1976?

87) _____ Who is considered the "other forward" and the "other Johnson" for Milwaukee? He is good enough, however, to have scored 15.4 points a game over a seven-year career.

88) _____ Who is the Buck who is ranked in the top ten free shooters of all time?

89) _____ Who is the Milwaukee shot-blocker who has never averaged five points a game in a seven-year pro career?

90) _____ Who is the Net, then with Kansas City, who sank 14 shots in a row in 1980–81? He averaged over 20 points a game from 1978–79 to 1980–81.

91) _____ Who is the former 20-point scorer for the champion (1976–77) Portland Trail Blazers who now mans the corner for the Knicks?

92) _____ Who was the Net rookie of 1980–81 who came within two assists of leading the club in that department?

93) _____ Who is the Laker who at one point during his career averaged 30 points a game for three consecutive years?

94) _____ Who is the present-day player who has scored more points in one season (2,831) than any other contemporary player?

13

95) _____ Who is the 7-foot, 20-point scorer for the Knicks who blocked just 83 shots in 82 games in 1980–81?

96) _____ Who is the Knick guard who led the NBA in steals and assists in 1979–80?

97) _____ Who is the player whom the Knicks traded after scoring 20.3 for 1979–80 and 1980–81?

98) _____ Who is the Knick who was second in turn-overs (302) to Moses Malone (308) in 1980–81?

99) _____ Who is the forward whom the Knicks suspended in 1981–82?

100) _____ Who is the Knick who in two seasons with the Nets averaged better than 20 points a game each year?

101) _____ Who got his middle name when his father named him after Roy Campanella, the great catcher?

102) _____ Who is the Hawk who in his first four seasons never shot less than 52 percent?

103) _____ Who is the second part of the "Twin Towers" in New York. Bill Cartwright, we'll assume, is the first part.

104) _____ Who played in his 800th consecutive game in 1981–82?

105) _____ Who won three MVP titles in the ABA?

106) _____ Who is the 76er who jumped from high school right into the pros?

107) _____ Who in 1980–81, and again in 1981–82, became the first sixth man to be named to the All-Star team?

108) _____ Who is the 76er guard who took over the back-court spot from the injured Doug Collins in 1980–81?

109) _____ Who is the 76er who was named to the NBA All-Defensive First Team from 1976–77 to 1980–81?

110) _____ Who is the Sixer who in his three-year career has averaged six assists per game?

111) _____ Who is the Sixer—he possesses an 11-point career average—who has 12 years of experience in the pros?

112) _____ Who is the Sixer reserve who came off the bench to shoot better than 50 percent in each season since 1976–77?

113) _____ Who is the 76er who teamed with Johnny Davis in the back-court for the Trail Blazers in their 1976-77 championship season?

114) _____ Who is the 76er who led the ABA in blocked shots from 1974–76 and shares the ABA record for most shots blocked (12) in one game?

115) _____ Who is the Phoenix Sun who averaged just four points a game in high school but has made the NBA All-Star team in each of the last three years?

116) _____ Who is the Sun guard (switched from forward last year) who averaged 21.9 points per game through 1980–81?

117) _____ Who is the Sun who was named the playoff MVP in 1979?

118) _____ Who is the Phoenix courtman who played for Coach John MacLeod in both college and the pros?

119) _____ Who is the Phoenix power forward—he has scored more than 10,000 points in his pro career—who attended the same high school as pro football players Harold Carmichael and Ken Burrough?

120) _____ Who is the Phoenix forward who was picked up by the Suns as a free agent after being named the Western League's MVP in 1978–79?

121) _____ Who is the Phoenix back-courtman who was an All-America at Kentucky? He played for his dad in high school.

122) _____ Who is the Phoenix center who in 1978–79 became the first seven-footer to sink 80 percent of his foul shots?

123) _____ Who is the Portland guard who set a club record for assists (555) in his first pro season?

124) _____ Who is the Portland center—he averaged 16 points a game in his first two seasons—who was born in the Bahamas?

125) _____ Who is the Portland forward who averaged 20 points a game for the Nets in 1979–80, his rookie season?

126) _____ Who is the Blazer guard who not too long ago played in the Continental League?

127) _____ Who is the Portland forward who hit 12

of 16 shots against Philadelphia in the final game of the championship series in 1976–77?

128) _____ Who is the Portland guard who had a .511 field goal percentage in four years in the ABA and a .555 mark in four years in the NBA?

129) _____ Who is the "Battering Ram" who quit college after his freshman year to join the Spurs at 19? He has averaged double figures during his seven-year career.

130) _____ Who is the Spur who has twice led the league in blocked shots? In one of those years (1980–81) he averaged only 23 minutes of playing time.

131) _____ Who has the longest active-game playing streak for the Spurs?

132) _____ Who is George Johnson's counterpart at center for San Antonio? The first player gives the Spurs defense; this player, offense.

133) _____ Who wears uniform number "00" for the Spurs?

134) _____ Who was the only NBA rookie non-starter in 1980–81 to lead his club in both steals and assists?

135) _____ Who was the backup to Bill Walton at UCLA who won the rebounding title in 1970–80 and finished second in 1980–81? He has been a solid double-digit scorer during his nine years in the pros.

136) _____ Who is the Clipper guard—he has scored almost 10,000 career points—who twice made the All-Star team when he played for Golden State?

137) _____ Who is the Clipper back-courtman—he averaged 19.3 points a game in 1980–81—who averaged 45 three-point field goals in 1979–80 and 1980–81?

138) _____ Who is the Clipper back-courtman—a veteran of ten years in the league—who sank a record (NBA) 90 three-point field goals in 1979–80?

139) _____ Who is the Clipper 12-year veteran whose 35-foot shot at the buzzer sent Phoenix into a third overtime period against the Celtics in the 1975–76 finals?

140) _____ Who is the Seattle center who made the league's All-Rookie team in 1978–79, played on a league championship club in 1978–79, and made the All-Star team in 1981–82?

114) _____ Who is the SuperSonic forward, a veteran of 12 NBA campaigns, who has averaged approximately 13 points a game in a career that has included stops in Cleveland, Portland, and Houston?

142) _____ Who is the Rutgers product who now plays forward for the Nets? He averaged 14 points a game for Seattle in 1980–81.

143) _____ Who has played his entire career, 12 years, in Seattle, during which time he has scored more than 12,000 points, some of them coming as one of the best three-point field goal shooters in the league?

144) _____ Who was the six-points-a-game career scorer at Notre Dame whom Seattle picked as its first-round draft choice in 1980?

145) _____ Who is the player who was a bust as a 6-8 center in New York but is a find as a power forward in Seattle?

146) _____ Who is the West Coast forward who played on teams that reached the finals in three of his first four years?

147) _____ Who is the three-time NBA All-Star First Team product who averaged 20 points a game for five (1976–80) consecutive seasons?

148) _____ Who is the Jazz forward who scored his 10,000th point midway through his sixth season?

149) _____ Who is the Jazz guard, a Louisville product, who was named the Most Outstanding Player in the 1980 NCAA Tournament?

150) _____ Who is the Utah forward who averaged more assists per game than any other forward in the league in 1980–81?

151) _____ Who is the Bullet forward who did not miss a game from 1978–79 to 1980–81?

152) _____ Who is the Washington back-courtman who averaged 40 three-pointers a year in 1979–80 and 1980–81?

153) _____ Who is the Bullet, a ten-year veteran, who has averaged approximately 13 points a game during stops that have included Los Angeles during its 1979–80 championship season?

154) _____ Who is the 1980–81 rookie who became the heir to Wes Unseld's job?

2. THE NBA IN CAPITAL LETTERS

Close followers of the NBA should romp to an easy victory in this quiz. We're going to provide you with the initials of five players—two guards, a center, and two forwards—from each team. (Some of the players could, if called upon, play more than one position.) All that you have to do is to identify the players.

New York Knicks		Houston Rockets	
M.R.R.	_____	C.M.	_____
R.S.	_____	M.D.	_____
B.C.	_____	M.M.	_____
M.L.	_____	E.H.	_____
C.R.	_____	R.R.	_____

Philadelphia 76ers		Denver Nuggets	
M.C.	_____	D.T.	_____
L.H.	_____	T.R.D.	_____
D.D.	_____	D.I.	_____
J.E.	_____	A.E.	_____
C.J.	_____	K.V.	_____

Boston Celtics		Kansas City Kings	
N.A.	_____	P.F.	_____
C.F.	_____	M.W.	_____
R.P.	_____	L.D.	_____
L.B.	_____	R.K.	_____
C.M.	_____	J.L.	_____

New Jersey Nets

O.B. _____
R.W. _____
B.W. _____
M.O'K. _____
J.B. _____

Washington Bullets

K.G. _____
J.L. _____
R.M. _____
G.B. _____
J.C. _____

Detroit Pistons

I.T. _____
J.L. _____
K.B. _____
K.T. _____
T.T. _____

Chicago Bulls

R.L. _____
R.T. _____
A.G. _____
J.W. _____
D.G. _____

Milwaukee Bucks

O.B. _____
S.M. _____
B.L. _____
M.J. _____
M.J. _____

Utah Jazz

D.G. _____
R.G. _____
B.P. _____
A.D. _____
A.B. _____

Dallas Mavericks

J.S. _____
R.B. _____
T.L. _____
M.A. _____
B.R. _____

Phoenix Suns

D.J. _____
W.D. _____
A.A. _____
L.R. _____
J.C. _____

Portland Trail Blazers

J.P. _____
K.R. _____
M.T. _____
C.N. _____
B.G. _____

Los Angeles Lakers

M.J. _____
N.N. _____
K.A.-J. _____
J.W. _____
M.K. _____

Atlanta Hawks

E.J.   ———
R.S.   ———
W.R.   ———
J.D.   ———
D.R.   ———

Indiana Pacers

D.B.   ———
J.D.   ———
H.W.   ———
L.O.   ———
B.K.   ———

Cleveland Cavaliers

G.H.   ———
B.W.   ———
J.E.   ———
K.C.   ———
R.W.   ———

San Antonio Spurs

G.G.   ———
J.M.   ———
D.C.   ———
M.M.   ———
M.O.   ———

Seattle SuperSonics

F.B.   ———
G.W.   ———
J.S.   ———
L.S.   ———
D.V.   ———

Golden State Warriors

L.F.   ———
P.S.   ———
J.B.C.   ———
B.K.   ———
L.S.   ———

San Diego Clippers

P.S.   ———
B.T.   ———
S.N.   ———
M.B.   ———
J.B.   ———

3. SEASON ASSIST LEADERS

Can you provide the season assist leader for each present-day team in the NBA? Two players may be used three times, and one player may be used twice. The respective teams and numbers of assists are provided. Records of clubs that preceded the present-day franchises count.

1) Atlanta Hawks _____ (679)
2) Boston Celtics _____ (715)
3) Chicago Bulls _____ (908)
4) Cleveland Cavaliers _____ (628)
5) Dallas Mavericks _____ (385)
6) Denver Nuggets _____ (610)
7) Detroit Pistons _____ (1,099)
8) Golden State Warriors _____ (846)
9) Houston Rockets _____ (768)
10) Indiana Pacers _____ (689)
11) Kansas City Kings _____ (910)
12) Los Angeles Lakers _____ (747)
13) Milwaukee Bucks _____ (668)
14) New Jersey Nets _____ (801)
15) New York Knicks _____ (832)
16) Philadelphia 76ers _____ (702)
17) Phoenix Suns _____ (605)
18) Portland Trail Blazers _____ (555)
19) San Antonio Spurs _____ (473)
20) San Diego Clippers _____ (663)
21) Seattle SuperSonics _____ (766)
22) Utah Jazz _____ (488)
23) Washington Bullets _____ (734)

4. SEASON REBOUND LEADERS

Can you provide the season rebound leader for each present-day team in the NBA? One player may be used three times, and one player may be used twice. The respective teams and numbers of rebounds are provided. Records of previous franchises count.

1) Atlanta Hawks _____ (1,540)
2) Boston Celtics _____ (1,930)
3) Chicago Bulls _____ (1,133)
4) Cleveland Cavaliers _____ (891)
5) Dallas Mavericks _____ (665)
6) Denver Nuggets _____ (1,637)
7) Detroit Pistons _____ (1,205)
8) Golden State Warriors _____ (2,149)
9) Houston Rockets _____ (1,444)
10) Indiana Pacers _____ (1,475)
11) Kansas City Kings _____ (1,688)
12) Los Angeles Lakers _____ (1,712)
13) Milwaukee Bucks _____ (1,346)
14) New Jersey Nets _____ (1,035)
15) New York Knicks _____ (1,191)
16) Philadelphia 76ers _____ (1,957)
17) Phoenix Suns _____ (1,015)
18) Portland Trail Blazers _____ (967)
19) San Antonio Spurs _____ (1,279)
20) San Diego Clippers _____ (1,184)
21) Seattle SuperSonics _____ (1,007)
22) Utah Jazz _____ (1,288)
23) Washington Bullets _____ (1,500)

5. SEASON SCORING LEADERS

Can you provide the season scoring leader for each present-day team in the NBA? Two players may be used twice. The respective teams and numbers of points are provided. Records of previous franchises count.

1) Atlanta Hawks   _____ (2,429)
2) Boston Celtics   _____ (2,388)
3) Chicago Bulls   _____ (2,403)
4) Cleveland Cavaliers   _____ (2,012)
5) Dallas Mavericks   _____ (1,184)
6) Denver Nuggets   _____ (2,519)
7) Detroit Pistons   _____ (2,213)
8) Golden State Warriors _____ (4,029)
9) Houston Rockets   _____ (2,350)
10) Indiana Pacers   _____ (2,353)
11) Kansas City Kings   _____ (2,719)
12) Los Angeles Lakers   _____ (2,538)
13) Milwaukee Bucks   _____ (2,822)
14) New Jersey Nets   _____ (2,518)
15) New York Knicks   _____ (2,303)
16) Philadelphia 76ers   _____ (2,649)
17) Phoenix Suns   _____ (2,048)
18) Portland Trail Blazers _____ (2,031)
19) San Antonio Spurs   _____ (2,585)
20) San Diego Clippers   _____ (2,831)
21) Seattle SuperSonics   _____ (2,251)
22) Utah Jazz   _____ (2,452)
23) Washington Bullets   _____ (2,495)

6. CAREER HIGHS

At the end of the 1981 season, there were 19 players in the NBA who had scored 50 or more points in a regular-season game. How many of them can you name?

1) _____	11) _____
2) _____	12) _____
3) _____	13) _____
4) _____	14) _____
5) _____	15) _____
6) _____	16) _____
7) _____	17) _____
8) _____	18) _____
9) _____	19) _____
10) _____	

7. PLAYOFF HIGHS

At the end of the 1981 season, there were 13 current-day players who had scored 40 or more points in a playoff game. How many of them can you name?

1) _____	8) _____
2) _____	9) _____
3) _____	10) _____
4) _____	11) _____
5) _____	12) _____
6) _____	13) _____
7) _____	

8. .500 CAREER SHOOTERS?

In the pairs of players listed below one of the players is over .500 percent as a career shooter, and one of them is under .500. Mark a check before the names of the players who are over.

1) __ Kareem Abdul-Jabbar	__ Dennis Johnson
2) __ Charlie Criss	__ Otis Birdsong
3) __ Adrian Dantley	__ Larry Kenon
4) __ Michael Richardson	__ Brad Davis
5) __ Walter Davis	__ Caldwell Jones
6) __ Darryl Dawkins	__ Fred Brown
7) __ Ben Poquette	__ Julius Erving
8) __ Artis Gilmore	__ Jim Chones
9) __ Bob Gross	__ Tom McMillen
10) __ Jack Sikma	__ Marques Johnson
11) __ Jim Brewer	__ Bobby Jones
12) __ Bernard King	__ Junior Bridgeman
13) __ Billy Knight	__ Ron Lee
14) __ Mitch Kupchak	__ Bill Robinzine
15) __ Reggie Theus	__ Bob Lanier
16) __ Moses Malone	__ Brian Taylor
17) __ David Greenwood	__ Cornbread Maxwell
18) __ Norm Nixon	__ Mack Calvin
19) __ Tom Owens	__ Mark Olberding
20) __ Phil Smith	__ Paul Westphal
21) __ Chris Ford	__ Swen Nater
22) __ George Gervin	__ Harvey Catchings
23) __ Wayne Rollins	__ Kevin Porter
24) __ Sidney Wicks	__ Robert Parish
25) __ Clifford Ray	__ Robert Reid

9. SUB-20-POINT-A-GAME SCORERS

Which of the following players have never averaged 20 points a game during their pro careers: Alvan Adams, Otis Birdsong, Junior Bridgeman, Fred Brown, Alex English, Phil Ford, Lionel Hollins, Dan Issel, Dennis Johnson, Eddie Johnson, Mickey Johnson, Larry Kenon, Billy Knight, Maurice Lucas, John Long, Calvin Murphy, Swen Nater, Mike Newlin, Billy Paultz, Len Robinson, Dave Robisch, Dan Roundfield, Randy Smith, Brian Taylor, Reggie Theus, Scott Wedman, Paul Westphal, Sidney Wicks, Ray Williams, and Brian Winters.

1) _____   9) _____
2) _____   10) _____
3) _____   11) _____
4) _____   12) _____
5) _____   13) _____
6) _____   14) _____
7) _____   15) _____
8) _____

10. 20-POINT (SEASON) PLAYOFF AVERAGES

Twenty of the listed players, going into the 1981–82 season, had a season playoff average of 20-or-more points a game. Which ones? Mark a check before each name that is correct.

1) __ Kareem Abdul-Jabbar
2) __ Nate Archibald
3) __ Billy Ray Bates
4) __ Larry Bird
5) __ Fred Brown
6) __ Tom Burleson
7) __ Doug Collins
8) __ Bob Dandridge
9) __ Walter Davis
10) __ John Drew
11) __ Julius Erving
12) __ George Gervin
13) __ Kevin Grevey
14) — Elvin Hayes
15) __ Dan Issel
16) __ Dennis Johnson
17) __ Marques Johnson
18) __ Mickey Johnson
19) __ Larry Kenon
20) __ Bernard King
21) __ Reggie King
22) __ Bob Lanier
23) __ Maurice Lucas
24) __ Moses Malone
25) __ Bob McAdoo
26) __ George McGinnis
27) __ Calvin Murphy
28) __ Campy Russell
29) __ Phil Smith
30) __ Randy Smith
31) __ David Thompson
32) __ Mychal Thompson
33) __ Rudy Tomjanovich
34) __ Scott Wedman
35) __ Paul Westphal
36) __ Jo Jo White
37) __ Jamaal Wilkes
38) __ Ray Williams
39) __ John Lee Williamson
40) __ Brian Winters

11. 25-POINT-PLUS SCORERS

Sixteen of the listed players averaged more than 25 points a game during their college careers. Mark a check before the names of those who did.

1) __ Kareem Abdul-Jabbar
2) __ Mike Gminski
3) __ Dan Issel
4) __ Don Buse
5) __ Norm Nixon
6) __ Julius Erving
7) __ Elvin Hayes
8) __ Kent Benson
9) __ Kevin Porter
10) __ Bob McAdoo
11) __ Bernard King
12) __ Calvin Murphy
13) __ Larry Bird
14) __ Maurice Lucas
15) __ Kevin Grevey

16) __ Austin Carr
17) __ Freeman Williams
18) __ Alvan Adams
19) __ Nate Archibald
20) __ Mike Mitchell
21) __ Adrian Dantley
22) __ Bob Lanier
23) __ Otis Birdsong
24) __ Dennis Awtrey
25) __ John Drew
26) __ George McGinnis
27) __ Bobby Jones
28) __ Mickey Johnson
29) __ George Gervin
30) __ Fred Brown

12. HITTING THE OPEN MAN

All of the players who are listed below can hit the open man. Twenty-one of them have recorded 480-or-more assists in one season. That breaks down to an average of approximately six assists a game for an 82-contest season. Which ones? Mark a check before the names of those who have.

___ Kareem Abdul-Jabbar
___ Alvan Adams
___ Nate Archibald
___ Henry Bibby
___ Larry Bird
___ Ron Boone
___ Mike Bratz
___ Fred Brown
___ Quinn Buckner
___ Don Buse
___ Mack Calvin
___ Maurice Cheeks
___ Johnny Davis
___ Julius Erving
___ Phil Ford
___ Tom Henderson
___ Armond Hill
___ Marques Johnson
___ Magic Johnson
___ Eddie Johnson

___ John Johnson
___ Allen Leavell
___ John Lucas
___ Jim McElroy
___ Mike Newlin
___ Norm Nixon
___ Kevin Porter
___ Michael Ray Richardson
___ James Silas
___ Randy Smith
___ Ricky Sobers
___ Brian Taylor
___ Reggie Theus
___ Wally Walker
___ Paul Westphal
___ Jo Jo White
___ Sidney Wicks
___ Bobby Wilkerson
___ Ray Williams
___ Brian Winters

13. THE HACKERS

One-half (26) of the players listed below have had a season-high number of disqualifications in excess of 10. (All of them have had at least eight dismissals in their worst "defensive" season.) Which ones? Mark a check before their names.

1) __ Kareem Abdul-Jabbar
2) __ Alvan Adams
3) __ James Bailey
4) __ John Brown
5) __ Joe Barry Carroll
6) __ Darryl Dawkins
7) __ Larry Demic
8) __ Coby Dietrick
9) __ Leon Douglas
10) __ John Drew
11) __ James Edwards
12) __ Lloyd Free
13) __ George Gervin
14) __ Paul Griffin
15) __ Steve Hawes
16) __ Elvin Hayes
17) __ Armond Hill
18) __ Phil Hubbard
19) __ Gus Johnson
20) __ Mickey Johnson
21) __ Caldwell Jones
22) __ Dwight Jones
23) __ Rich Kelley
24) __ Bernard King
25) __ Kevin Kunnert
26) __ Sam Lacey

27) __ Ron Lee
28) __ Scott Lloyd
29) __ George McGinnis
30) __ Tom McMillen
31) __ Joe Meriweather
32) __ Steve Mix
33) __ Calvin Murphy
34) __ Mike O'Koren
35) __ Tom Owens
36) __ Robert Parish
37) __ Ben Poquette
38) __ Kevin Porter
39) __ Clifford Ray
40) __ Robert Reid
41) __ Bill Robinzine
42) __ Wayne Rollins
43) __ Dan Roundfield
44) __ Lonnie Shelton
45) __ Larry Smith
46) __ Ricky Sobers
47) __ Mychal Thompson
48) __ Jan van Breda Kolff
49) __ Kermit Washington
50) __ Richard Lee Washington
51) __ Scott Wedman
52) __ Sidney Wicks

14. 1981 COLLEGE DRAFT

The players listed below were first-round and second-round choices in the 1981 NBA college draft. Mark 1 next to the first-round pick and 2 next to the others.

1) __ Mark Aguirre
2) __ Tracy Jackson
3) __ Danny Ainge
4) __ Isiah Thomas
5) __ Albert King
6) __ Jeff Lamp
7) __ Gene Banks
8) __ Jay Vincent
9) __ Dan Schayes
10) __ Brian Jackson
11) __ Howard Wood
12) __ Buck Williams
13) __ Danny Vranes
14) __ Eddie Johnson
15) __ Orlando Woolridge
16) __ Clyde Bradshaw
17) __ Greg Cook
18) __ Kelly Tripucka
19) __ Sam Williams
20) __ Herb Williams
21) __ Ray Blume
22) __ Mike McGee
23) __ Tom Chambers
24) __ Charles Davis
25) __ Ed Turner

15. HIGH AND LOW

One-half of the following players were first-round picks; one-half weren't selected until at least the fourth round: Henry Bibby, Mike Bantom, Hawkeye Whitney, Michael Carr, Winford Boynes, Cookie Cook, Bob Dandridge, Rickey Brown, Ron Davis, Dave Corzine, Brad Davis, Mike Evans, Mike Dunleavy, Phil Ford, Roy Hamilton, Paul Griffin, George Johnson, Mickey Johnson, John Lambert, Billy McKinney, Steve Mix, Tom McMillen, James Ray, Frankie Sanders, Al Scott, Wally Walker, Randy Smith, and Mike Woodson. Put the correct names in each category.

First-Round
1) _____
2) _____
3) _____
4) _____
5) _____
6) _____
7) _____
8) _____
9) _____
10) _____
11) _____
12) _____
13) _____
14) _____

Low-Round
1) _____
2) _____
3) _____
4) _____
5) _____
6) _____
7) _____
8) _____
9) _____
10) _____
11) _____
12) _____
13) _____
14) _____

16. FIRST, SECOND, AND DOWN THE LIST

Eleven of the following players were first-round picks, eleven of them were second-round choices, and nine of them were the 96th-or-above player to be selected. Place them in their proper columns.

Kareem Abdul-Jabbar
Ron Boone
Marvin Barnes
Mack Calvin
Otis Birdsong
Jim Brewer
Kent Benson
Phil Ford
Dave Greenwood
Austin Carr
Joe Barry Carroll
Mike Dunleavy
Doug Collins
Artis Gilmore
Dan Issel
Darrell Griffith

Elvin Hayes
Magic Johnson
Scott May
Bob Lanier
Allen Leavell
Bob McAdoo
John Lucas
David Thompson
Rudy Tomjanovich
Billy Paultz
Randy Smith
Wes Unseld
Sidney Wicks
John Williamson
Mychal Thompson

First-Round	Second-Round	Down the List
1) _____	1) _____	1) _____
2) _____	2) _____	2) _____
3) _____	3) _____	3) _____
4) _____	4) _____	4) _____
5) _____	5) _____	5) _____
6) _____	6) _____	6) _____
7) _____	7) _____	7) _____
8) _____	8) _____	8) _____
9) _____	9) _____	9) _____
10) _____	10) _____	
11) _____	11) _____	

17. PLAYER POSITIONS

Forty current-day players are listed below. All you have to do is to write their positions—"Guard," "Forward," or "Center"—next to their names. If you're a "pro," you're going to fast-break your opponents right off the floor in this game.

1) Alvan Adams _____
2) James Bailey _____
3) Otis Birdsong _____
4) Don Buse _____
5) Dave Corzine _____
6) John Drew _____
7) Chris Ford _____
8) Mike Gminski _____
9) Kevin Grevey _____
10) Steve Hawes _____
11) Mickey Johnson _____
12) Caldwell Jones _____
13) Bobby Jones _____
14) Mitch Kupchak _____
15) Tom Lagarde _____
16) Bill Laimbeer _____
17) John Long _____
18) Maurice Lucas _____
19) Cornbread Maxwell _____
20) Sidney Moncrief _____
21) Mike Newlin _____
22) Mike O'Koren _____
23) Robert Parish _____
24) Billy Paultz _____
25) Jim Paxson _____
26) Roger Phegley _____
27) Robert Reid _____

28) Rick Robey _____
29) Truck Robinson _____
30) Dave Robisch _____
31) John Roche _____
32) Jack Sikma _____
33) James Silas _____
34) Phil Smith _____
35) Brian Taylor _____
36) Jan van Breda Kolff _____
37) Marvin Webster _____
38) Richard Washington _____
39) Sly Williams _____
40) Bill Willoughby _____

18. CURRENT NBA NUMBERS

Match the following present-day players with the numbers (in parentheses below) that they have made recognizable in NBA play: Scott May, Darrell Griffith, Eddie Johnson, Dave Corzine, Jim Spanarkel, Nate Archibald, Don Buse, Len Elmore, Geoff Huston, Moses Malone, Lloyd Free, Larry Bird, Robert Parish, Alex English, Kevin Porter, Abdul Jeelani, Bob Lanier, John Drew, Marques Johnson, Greg Ballard, Lorenzo Romar, Joe Bryant, Charlie Criss, Lionel Hollins, Ray Williams (Knicks), Norm Nixon, John Long, John Johnson, Adrian Dantley, Sidney Moncrief, Billy Paultz, Jim Paxson, Julius Erving, Phil Ford, Billy Ray Bates, Gus Williams, Wayne Rollins, Kareem Abdul-Jabbar, Bernard King, Jack Sikma, Dan Issel, Mike O'Koren, Magic Johnson, George Gervin, Mickey Johnson, James Wilkes, Dan Roundfield, Kiki Vandeweghe, Steve Mix, Bill Robinzine, Tom McMillen, Joe C. Meriweather, Artis Gilmore, Jamaal Wilkes, and Darryl Dawkins.

1) _____ (00)		15) _____ (10)	
2) _____ (1)		16) _____ (10)	
3) _____ (1)		17) _____ (11)	
4) _____ (1)		18) _____ (12)	
5) _____ (2)		19) _____ (13)	
6) _____ (3)		20) _____ (14)	
7) _____ (4)		21) _____ (16)	
8) _____ (4)		22) _____ (17)	
9) _____ (4)		23) _____ (18)	
10) _____ (5)		24) _____ (20)	
11) _____ (6)		25) _____ (21)	
12) _____ (7)		26) _____ (22)	
13) _____ (8)		27) _____ (23)	
14) _____ (9)		28) _____ (24)	

29) _____ (25)   43) _____ (42)
30) _____ (27)   44) _____ (43)
31) _____ (30)   45) _____ (43)
32) _____ (30)   46) _____ (44)
33) _____ (31)   47) _____ (44)
34) _____ (32)   48) _____ (50)
35) _____ (32)   49) _____ (50)
36) _____ (32)   50) _____ (52)
37) _____ (33)   51) _____ (53)
38) _____ (33)   52) _____ (53)
39) _____ (34)   53) _____ (54)
40) _____ (35)   54) _____ (54)
41) _____ (40)   55) _____ (55)
42) _____ (41)

19. BIG TRADES

Match the player(s) in the left-hand column with the player(s) in the right-hand column. They figured in significant trades.

1) __ Abdul-Jabbar and Wesley
2) __ Archibald, Barnes, and Knight
3) __ Dantley
4) __ Birdsong
5) __ Buse
6) __ Dantley (to Utah)
7) __ English
8) __ Erving and Sojourner
9) __ Free
10) __ Hayes
11) __ Issel
12) __ D. Johnson
13) __ B. Jones and Simpson
14) __ B. King
15) __ Lanier
16) __ McAdoo
17) __ Newlin
18) __ K. Porter
19) __ Foots Walker
20) __ Westphal

a) Robisch
b) C. Scott
c) C. Robinson
d) Sobers
e) Phegley
f) McGinnis
g) P. Smith
h) Marin
i) Haywood
j) McGinnis (from Denver)
k) Knight
l) Benson
m) W. Cooper
n) Woodson
o) Westphal
p) Bing
q) Gianelli
r) George Carter and K. Washington
s) Smith, Winters, Meyers, and Bridgeman
t) Washington, Kunnert, and Wicks

20. DID THEY OR DIDN'T THEY?

Did the players who are listed below play on a championship club in the NBA or didn't they? Mark a check before those who did. There are 19 in all.

1) __ Nate Archibald
2) __ Henry Bibby
3) __ Lloyd Free
4) __ Mike Cooper
5) __ John Long
6) __ Reggie Theus
7) __ David Thompson
8) __ Jack Sikma
9) __ Mitch Kupchak
10) __ Fred Brown
11) __ Ronnie Lester
12) __ Leonard Elmore
13) __ Norm Nixon
14) __ Quinn Buckner
15) __ Artis Gilmore
16) __ Steve Mix
17) __ Elvin Hayes
18) __ Bob Gross
19) __ John Drew
20) __ Charlie Criss
21) __ Lionel Hollins

22) __ Dennis Johnson
23) __ Campy Russell
24) __ Terry Tyler
25) __ Phil Smith
26) __ Toby Knight
27) __ Darryl Dawkins
28) __ Rick Robey
29) __ Lonnie Shelton
30) __ Bob Lanier
31) __ Michael Ray Richardson
32) __ Sly Williams
33) __ Robert Parish
34) __ Paul Westphal
35) __ Jim Chones
36) __ Gus Williams
37) __ Robert Reid
38) __ Mark Olberding
39) __ Cornbread Maxwell
40) __ Dennis Awtrey

21. LAST NAMES

Can you provide the (last) names that correspond with the first names of the present-day players? (In some cases there are more than one player with the first names listed. In the Answers only one last name is given.)

1) Winford _____
2) Dudley _____
3) Ulysses _____
4) Harvey _____
5) Coby _____
6) Eric _____
7) Garfield _____
8) Armond _____
9) Cedric _____
10) Clemon _____
11) Dwight _____
12) Toby _____
13) Roger _____
14) Clint _____
15) Lorenzo _____
16) DeWayne _____
17) Purvis _____
18) Carlos _____
19) Jan _____
20) Sylvester _____

22. THE RIGHT HEIGHT

The fifty current-day players who are listed below range in height from 5-8 to 7-2. They range in ability, too. But each of them stands tall in the pro ranks. Can you match them with their proper altitudes?

Nate Archibald
Artis Gilmore
Robert Parish
Phil Ford
Jim Chones
Kareem Abdul-Jabbar
Truck Robinson

Ed Jordan
Charlie Criss
Steve Mix
Elvin Hayes
Mike Newlin
Bobby Jones
Bob Lanier

Tom Burleson	Joe Barry Carroll
Kevin Porter	John Lucas
Jack Sikma	Mike Dunleavy
Brad Davis	Bob Dandridge
Bill Cartwright	Campy Russell
Dan Issel	Toby Knight
Alvan Adams	Maurice Cheeks
Lloyd Free	Chris Ford
Tree Rollins	George Gervin
Marvin Webster	Phil Hubbard
Michael Ray Richardson	Wes Matthews
Allan Bristow	Darrell Griffith
Adrian Dantley	James Edwards
Billy Knight	Rich Kelley
Joe Bryant	Johnny Davis
Calvin Murphy	Ken Higgs
John Drew	Jeff Wilkins
Steve Hawes	Paul Mokeski

7-0 to 7-2	6-8 to 6-11	6-4 to 6-7	6-0 to 6-3
1) _____	1) _____	1) _____	1) _____
2) _____	2) _____	2) _____	2) _____
3) _____	3) _____	3) _____	3) _____
4) _____	4) _____	4) _____	4) _____
5) _____	5) _____	5) _____	5) _____
6) _____	6) _____	6) _____	6) _____
7) _____	7) _____	7) _____	7) _____
8) _____	8) _____	8) _____	8) _____
9) _____	9) _____	9) _____	9) _____
10) _____	10) _____	10) _____	10) _____
11) _____	11) _____	11) _____	11) _____
12) _____	12) _____	12) _____	12) _____

Under 6

1) _____
2) _____

23. A WEIGHTY SUBJECT

All of the present-day players who are listed below are "big" men. Mark a check before the names of those who weigh 245-or-more pounds.

1) _____ Dennis Awtrey
2) _____ Kent Benson
3) _____ Bill Cartwright
4) _____ Dave Corzine
5) _____ Darryl Dawkins
6) _____ James Donaldson
7) _____ Ralph Drollinger
8) _____ Artis Gilmore
9) _____ Mike Gminski
10) _____ Elvin Hayes

11) _____ Dan Issel
12) _____ Clemon Johnson
13) _____ Rich Kelley
14) _____ Bob Lanier
15) _____ Rick Mahorn
16) _____ Paul Mokeski
17) _____ Swen Nater
18) _____ Billy Paultz
19) _____ Rick Robisch
20) _____ Marvin Webster

24. YOU BE THE REF

We often get mad at the referees, but we seldom remember their names. Below you will find a list of names in which are included present-day referees and former players. Can you differentiate between the two? Next to their names write either "R" for referees or "P" for players.

1) Ed Rush ___
2) Rick Adelman ___
3) Art Becker ___
4) Lee Jones ___
5) Jake O'Donnell ___
6) Fred Boyd ___
7) Earl Strom ___

8) Pete Cross ___
9) Jack Madden ___
10) Joe Crawford ___
11) Dick Duckett ___
12) Dan Finn ___
13) Ed Middleton ___
14) Mal Graham ___

15) Cleo Hill ___
16) Jim Capers ___
17) Jess Kersey ___
18) Kevin Joyce ___
19) Red Klotz ___
20) Paul Mihalak ___
21) Hugh Evans ___
22) Eddie Mast ___
23) Jack Molinas ___
24) Tom Nunez ___
25) Terry Durham ___
26) Bill Simmons ___
27) Chuck Noble ___

28) Tom O'Keefe ___
29) Jess Thompson ___
30) Jim Phelan ___
31) Bob Riley ___
32) Zeke Sinicola ___
33) Jack Nies ___
34) Charles Tyra ___
35) Gene Vance ___
36) Blane Reichelt ___
37) Barry Rogan ___
38) Hue Hollins ___
39) Luke Witte ___
40) Matt Zunic ___

25. PRO POTPOURRI

1) _____ Who made 67 percent of his shots in 1980–81?

2) _____ What Bull has never missed an NBA game?

3) _____ Whom did Don Delaney replace as coach of the Cavaliers?

4) _____ Who led the league in three-point attempts (169) in 1980–81?

5) _____ What coach recently jumped from a contender to an expansion team that lost 67 games?

6) _____ Whom did Doug Moe replace as the Nugget coach?

7) _____ What 1980–81 team led the league in offense and finished last in defense?

8) _____ Which team became the first one since the 1971–72 Warriors to have three players average 20 points a game?

9) _____ Who were the players?

_____
_____

43

10) _____ What team was the only one not to average 100 points a game in 1980–81?

11) _____ Who was the 1980–81 Comeback Player of the Year?

12) _____ Who was the Warriors' second-round draft choice who finished third in the league in rebounding in 1980–81?

13) _____ Who in 1980–81 missed just nine of 215 free throws?

14) _____ Who in 1980–81 finished first in rebounding and second in scoring?

15) _____ Who was the 1980–81 seven-footer who averaged just seven rebounds a game?

16) _____ Who finished out the season as coach after Kevin Loughery resigned with the Nets?

17) _____ Who was the Nets' leading scorer in 1980–81 whom they traded after the season?

18) _____ Who was their number-two scorer whom they also traded?

19) _____ Who was the Knick who finished fourth in assists and second in steals in 1980–81?

20) _____ What team tied a record by winning 37 of its 41 games at home?

21) _____ Who is regarded as the most versatile and valuable reserve in the NBA?

22) _____ Who is the Trail Blazer who was picked up from the Continental League in 1980?

23) _____ Who became the first non-center in 17 years to win the MVP Award?

24) _____ What SuperSonic player sat out the entire year in a contract dispute?

25) _____ Whom did the SuperSonics trade to Phoenix for Paul Westphal?

26) _____ What team had the league's leading scorer and the Rookie of the Year in 1980–81?

27) _____ Who shot a runner-up .935 from the free throw line?

28) _____ Who, in addition to Artis Gilmore, shot .600 (.607) from the floor?

29) _____ Who led the league in three-point shooting percentage (.383) in 1980–81?

30) _____ Who sank the most (57) three-point field goals?

31) _____ Who was the runner-up with 53 three-point field goals?

32) _____ Who is the present-day player who made the All-League Defensive Team in all four of his years (1973–76) in the ABA?

THE 24-SECOND RULE

How did the 24-second rule come into being?

Well, the Fort Wayne Pistons of 1950–51, under the direction of Coach Murray Mendenhall, get a large measure of the credit for the rule change. Early in the season the Pistons traveled to Minneapolis where they were scheduled to meet the Lakers on a smaller-than-standard floor. The Lakers were big and slow, so the court was ideal for the host team.

Mendenhall had two points to prove that night. First, he wanted to break the Lakers' string of 29 consecutive home-court victories, and, second, he wanted to publicize his complaint that Minneapolis used an illegal zone defense. He decided to play a slow-down game.

The game became a virtual stalemate. The Pistons held the ball and the Lakers refused to pressure the ball. At the end of the first quarter, the Pistons led, 8–7. By halftime the Lakers rallied to take a two–point lead, 13–11.

The Minneapolis fans were incensed. They showered the Fort Wayne players and coach with verbal and physical abuse. The Piston bench area was littered with debris.

But Fort Wayne was not deterred from following its game plan. Going into the fourth period, the Lakers held tenaciously to a slim one-point (17–16) lead. In the first eight minutes of the final period, each team scored only one foul shot. Then the Pistons, trailing 18–17, went into a four-minute freeze, holding the ball for the last shot. Larry Foust sank a hook shot, with ten seconds remaining in the game, to give Fort Wayne a 19–18 victory in the NBA's lowest scoring game.

Shortly afterwards, Danny Biasone, the owner of the Syracuse Nationals, suggested a time limit. He had done some research. Twenty-four seconds, he said, seemed like enough time for a team to get off a shot. That's how the rule came into effect.

In that unprecedented game, interestingly enough, six Piston players scored at least two points. John Oldham led them with five points. Only three players scored for Minneapolis, though. George Mikan took game scoring honors with 15 points. Bob Harrison converted on both of his foul tries, and Jim Pollard sank his only shot from the charity-stripe line.

The Pistons had three assists; the Lakers, four. One of the Laker assists was recorded by a player who was not used to scoring many points. But he has become used to recording many victories as the coach of a National Football League team.

Who was that somewhat obscure NBA player who went on to become one of the more recognizable NFL coaches?

Answer: Bud Grant of the Minnesota Vikings

FIRST PERIOD SCORE

Points
You __ The NBA __
Games
You __ The NBA __

THE
SECOND
QUARTER

26. COURT CHRONOLOGY I

Fill in the blanks.

1) _____ By whom was the idea of a big-city professional basketball league first suggested?

2) _____ Who was the president of the Boston Garden who liked the idea?

3) _____ Who was the representative of Madison Square Garden who muscled the league's "brain child" out of the picture?

4) _____ What league did they formulate in June, 1946?

5) _____ Whom did they name the first commissioner of the league?

6) _____ Who was the Philadelphia owner, one of the few team magnates who had a basketball background?

7) _____ Who, in the NBL, signed the first big contract, a five-year pact worth $60,000?

8) _____ Who was the former high school coach who was named the head mentor of the Washington Capitols?

9) _____ What team, in that first season, ran off a 17-game winning streak en route to winning the Eastern Division championship?

10) _____ Who was the league's first standout scorer? He led the runner-up by almost seven points a game.

11) _____ Who scored a record 63 points in a 1949 contest against Indianapolis?

12) _____ Who was the first coach of the Celtics?

13) _____ How many games did each team play in that first year?

14) _____ In 1947 the schedule was cut to how many games?

15) _____ How many games do the present-day teams play?

16) _____ What team won the league's first official championship?

17) _____ What expansion team won the league championship the following (1947–48) year?

18) _____ From what NBL team did the Minneapolis Lakers draft George Mikan in 1947–48?

19) _____ Who came to Minneapolis from the same defunct team? (He and the preceding player made the NBL All-Star team as the Lakers won the league championship.)

20) _____ Who was the Laker owner who nailed the lid on the NBL's coffin when he jumped to the BAA with his team? (He currently owns the NFL's Minnesota Vikings.)

27. COURT CHRONOLOGY II

Fill in the blanks.

1) _____ The merger between the NBL and the BAA led to the formation of what league?

2) _____ Who was the owner of Tri-Cities?

3) _____ Who was the owner of the Syracuse Nationals?

4) _____ What brothers owned the Royals?

5) _____ Who was the Rochester Royal player who made the All-Star team in the first year of the NBA?

6) _____ The fabulous players from the 1949–50 Kentucky Wildcats became player-owners of what pro team in 1950–51?

7) _____ What center from that team made first-team All-Pro in his first NBA season?

8) _____ What guard from that team made the first-team All-Pro club, too?

9) _____ Who was Red Auerbach's first draft choice as coach of the Celtics?

10) _____ What team first drafted Bob Cousy?

11) _____ Who was the Fort Wayne rookie who was banned from the league for betting on games?

12) _____ Who was the referee who admitted taking $3,000 to fix three games?

13) _____ Who was the first black player to be drafted by a professional basketball team?

14) _____ What black player did the Knicks purchase from the Harlem Globetrotters in the same year?

15) _____ Who was the 6-11 Bowling Green graduate whom Red Auerbach chose over Bob Cousy?

16) _____ To what team did Tri-Cities trade Cousy, before he had played even one pro game?

17) _____ Three weeks before the season opened, however, the franchise folded. The names of the club's three best players were put into a hat by the league commissioner and picked by the Knicks, the Warriors, and the Celtics. Whom did the Knicks get?

18) _____ Whom did the Warriors acquire?

19) _____ With whom were the Celtics "stuck?"

20) _____ The player whom the Celtics picked over Cousy in the draft never played for Boston. He was peddled to Fort Wayne because Red Auerbach was able to pick up the big center from St. Louis, which folded after the 1950 season. Who was that former St. Louis University player?

28. COURT CHRONOLOGY III

Fill in the blanks.

1) _____ Who was the former NYU player who held the career scoring mark in the NBA when he retired in 1964?

2) _____ The Knicks lost the preceding all-round forward because they underbid the Syracuse Nationals by what pittance?

3) _____ For whom did Fort Wayne trade Bob Cousy to Chicago?

4) _____ Who was the Warrior scoring champ who played with Joe Fulks and Neil Johnston, teammates, who also were scoring champs?

5) _____ Who was the Celtic who in a playoff series got into a fight with Dolph Schayes? (Both of the players were thrown out of the game in the opening minutes of the contest.)

6) _____ Who was the Celtic guard who, in 1953, scored a record 50 points in a playoff game that went four overtimes?

7) _____ By what team was Bill Russell drafted?

8) _____ Who was the principal player that Red Auerbach traded to the above team for Russell?

9) _____ Who was the "throw-in" that Boston gave up in the deal?

10) _____ Who was the territorial choice, a 6-7 forward from Holy Cross, whom Auerbach picked up in the same draft?

11) _____ Who was the college teammate of the "throw-in" in the Russell deal whom Auerbach had picked up in an earlier draft? (He became a great "sixth man.")

12) _____ Who was the Celtic who made a 70-foot shot in the 1956-57 All-Star Game?

13) _____ Who was the Royal rebounding star who was stricken with encephalitis?

14) _____ Who was the above player's teammate who became his legal guardian?

15) _____ Whose record 50 points (in regulation time) in the final playoff game of 1958 gave the Hawks the league championship?

16) _____ Who formerly held the regulation-game record in playoff competition?

17) _____ Which team was the first club to win four straight games in the playoff finals?

18) _____ Who, in 1960, broke Joe Fulks's one-game scoring record (63 points) with a total of 64 points?

19) _____ Who was the owner who was known as "The Mogul?"

20) _____ What high school player was a club's draft pick on the basis of the league's territorial ruling?

29. COURT CHRONOLOGY IV

Fill in the blanks.

1) _____ Who was the Knick coach who led St. John's to NIT titles before and after he coached in the pros?

2) _____ Who was the player who scored 78 points in a 1961–62 game that went three overtime periods?

3) _____ Who was the all-league player who scored 63 points in the same game?

4) _____ Later in that season a player set a new regulation-game record with 73 points. Who was he?

5) _____ Who was the Warrior guard who got 20

assists the night Wilt Chamberlain scored a league-record 100 points?

6) _____ Who succeeded Maurice Podoloff as the league commissioner?

7) _____ To whom did Bob Short sell the Lakers?

8) _____ Who became the youngest (24) coach in the league?

9) _____ In the Hawks's first 16 years they had 16 different head coaches. Which one of them led the Hawks on two different occasions?

10) _____ For whom did the Celtics wear a mourning band in 1965–66?

11) _____ Whose critical deflection in the final game of the 1965–66 semi-final playoffs against Philadelphia saved a one-point victory for the Celtics?

12) _____ Who in the finals of that year averaged 40 points a game in a losing effort to Boston?

13) _____ Who was the first black coach in the NBA?

14) _____ Who was the Philadelphia player who performed in the playoffs twenty years after his father represented the same city in the 1947 playoffs?

15) _____ Who scored 1,000 or more points in the most (16) seasons?

16) _____ Who was the first rookie to win the MVP Award?

17) _____ Who was the second player to perform the feat?

18) _____ With what team did the Milwaukee Bucks win the coin toss that enabled them to draft Lew Alcindor?

19) _____ Who was the only rookie of the year for the Knicks?

20) _____ Who was the Knick player whose career was interrupted by a heart attack?

30. COURT CHRONOLOGY V

Fill in the blanks.

1) _____ Who was the principal player whom the Knicks traded to Detroit for Dave DeBusschere?

2) _____ Who was the back-up player in the deal?

3) _____ What team rolled off a (then) record 18-game winning streak in 1970–71?

4) _____ Whose 55-foot shot at the buzzer forced an overtime period in a playoff game?

5) _____ Whose mere presence—he was hobbling from a leg injury—at the outset of the seventh game of the playoff finals inspired his team to win the league championship?

6) _____ Who played 47 consecutive complete games?

7) _____ Who scored a record 35 consecutive field goals?

8) _____ Which "Coach of the Year" lost his voice as his team battled down the stretch of the league season?

9) _____ Who was the first player to lead the league in both assists and scoring in the same season?

10) _____ Who was named the playoff MVP in both of the years that his team won the league championship?

11) _____ Who was the first Commissioner of the ABA?

12) _____ What was the color of the ABA's ball?

13) _____ Who was the NBA player who jumped from the Syracuse Nationals in the officially recognized pro league to the Cleveland Pipers of the ABL?

14) _____ Who was technically the first black man to coach a professional basketball team? He led the Pipers.

15) _____ Who was the player—he never participated in a college game—who won the ABL's first-and-only scoring championship?

16) _____ Who was the founder of the ABL?
17) _____ Who was the most important ABA recruit?
18) _____ What team won the ABA's first championship?
19) _____ Who was the league's MVP?
20) _____ Who was the league's Coach of the Year?

31. COURT CHRONOLOGY VI

Fill in the blanks.

1) _____ Who was the Minnesota player who was named Rookie of the Year?
2) _____ Who was the player who sank an 88-foot shot in that maiden season?
3) _____ Who was the Pittsburgh coach who lost his job because he got into a fight with Piper owner Gabe Rubin?
4) _____ Who was the former teammate of Mikan who replaced the fired coach?
5) _____ Who succeeded Mikan as Commissioner?
6) _____ Who was the "must" college star whom the ABA failed to sign?
7) _____ Who was the important ABA star who defected to the NBA?
8) _____ Who won a $1.5 million law settlement with the NBA?
9) _____ Who led the league in scoring and rebounding while being voted Rookie of the Year and MVP?
10) _____ Who was the Kentucky Colonel player who won the Rookie of the Year and MVP awards in the same season?
11) _____ What ABA star was awarded to the NBA Warriors by the courts?

12) _____ What NBA 76er was awarded to the ABA Carolina Cougars?

13) _____ Who was the league star who was traded from the Squires to the Nets?

14) _____ Whom did the league pay $1.8 million in salary to be part owner, the coach, and a player for the San Diego Conquistadors?

15) _____ Who was the only All-League player in 1946–47 who had been a "big name" in college?

16) _____ Which team finished a season 29–1 at home?

17) _____ Pro basketball's playoffs were modeled on the playoff format of what other sport?

18) _____ Who was the player-coach of the 1947–48 Baltimore Bullets, the league's champions?

19) _____ Who was the 19-year-old Knick who scored a record 47 points in one game during the 1947–48 season?

20) _____ Who was the first pro basketball player to score 1,000 points in a season?

32. COURT CHRONOLOGY VII

Fill in the blanks.

1) _____ Who was the second player to perform the feat? He was the only player to score over 1,000 points during the shortened (48 games) 1947–48 season?

2) _____ In the 1948–49 season who scored a game-record 63 points?

3) _____ Who was the Tri-Cities Blackhawk who led the moribund NBL in scoring in 1948–49 with a 13.8 average?

4) _____ What team, in the first NBA season, won 37 of its 38 games at home?

5) _____ What team, during the same season, won 36 out of 38 games at home?

6) _____ Who was the Laker who decided Game One of the final playoffs with a 40-foot shot at the buzzer?

7) _____ Who was the Knick back-courtman who led the NBA in assists during its first year?

8) _____ What team did Auerbach coach in between stops in Washington and Boston?

9) _____ Who was the player whom Boston got when Washington folded during the 1950–51 season?

10) _____ Whose two free throws decided the final game of the 1950–51 playoffs between the victorious Rochester Royals and the New York Knicks?

11) _____ During the 1951–52 season a big front-courtman who made the All-League Team the preceding year was implicated in a college fixing scandal. Who was he?

12) _____ Who was his back-court teammate, also an all-league choice the preceding year, who was also dismissed from the professional ranks?

13) _____ To neutralize what big man did the league widen its foul lines to 12 feet?

14) _____ What was the original width?

15) _____ To neutralize the effectiveness of what other big man did the league widen its lanes to 16 feet?

16) _____ Who was the first guard to average 20 points a game for an entire season?

17) _____ Who was the first player to lead the league in assists in back-to-back years?

18) _____ Who was the medical student—now the club physician for the Lakers—who became a valuable sixth man for the Knicks? He is the father of a present-day player.

19) _____ Who was his brother-in-law, who led the league in rebounding in 1951–52?

20) _____ Who was the back-court scorer whom the Celtics acquired from Washington when the Capitols folded?

33. COURT CHRONOLOGY VIII

Fill in the blanks.

1) _____ Who converted 30 of 32 attempts from the foul line during a playoff game?

2) _____ The All-Star Team had three centers on the first team in the 1952–53 season. George Mikan was one; Ed Macauley was a second. Who was the third?

3) _____ Who was the Syracuse Nat forward who led the league in rebounds?

4) _____ Who was the Knick forward who led the league in rebounds?

5) _____ Who was the first player to lead the league in scoring for three consecutive years?

6) _____ Who was the first player to average 16 rebounds a game in one season?

7) _____ Who was the Syracuse player who helped the Nats win the league championship with a game-winning free throw and a game-saving steal against Fort Wayne in the final game of the 1954–55 playoff finals?

8) _____ Who was the Piston coach, a former referee, who pushed Syracuse to a seventh game in the 1954–55 finals?

9) _____ The Milwaukee Hawks boasted two outstanding first-year players in 1954–55. One was a 20.4 points-per-game forward out of Louisiana State. Who was he?

10) _____ The other was a 19.0 points-per-game guard out of Furman. (He once scored 100 points in a college game.) Who was he?

11) _____ In 1954–55 Philadelphia had the one-two league scorers. Johnston led the league. Who finished second?

12) _____ Who was the first player to lead the league in assists for three consecutive years?

13) _____ Who was the 6-5 forward who played guard under Piston Coach Charlie Eckman's "four big-man" alignment in 1955–56?

14) _____ In the same season a second-year player led the league in season's points and rebounds. Who was he?

15) _____ But a Royal rebounder, out of St. Francis of Loretta (Pa.), led the league in average number of rebounds (16.3) per game. Who was he?

16) _____ Who was the first rebounder to average over 17 rebounds a game?

17) _____ Whose ankle injury impaired the Celtics' strength in Boston's six-game loss to the Hawks in the 1957–58 playoff finals?

18) _____ Who paced the Hawks with 50 points—19 of them in the last quarter—in the wrap-up game?

19) _____ Who was the first player to score 2,000 points in a season?

20) _____Who took Mikan's place with Minneapolis?

34. COURT CHRONOLOGY IX

Fill in the blanks.

1) _____ Who concluded his career in Detroit with an iron-man streak of playing in 746 consecutive games? He earlier played for the Knicks.

2) _____ Who was the first player to average 20 rebounds a game?

3) _____ Who broke Mikan's record of scoring 28.4 points a game for a season?

4) _____ Who was the first rookie to make the All-Star Team?

5) _____ Who was the first courtman to be named Player of the Year?

6) _____ Who was the first player to win the honor a second time?

7) _____ Who scored 61 points in a double overtime game in 1952?

8) _____ Who scored 55 points as a rookie during the 1958–59 season?

9) _____ Which team had an 18-game winning streak against a team it faced in the 1958–59 season?

10) _____ Who scored 32 consecutive points without missing?

11) _____ Who was the 6-4 forward who averaged 23.7 points a game for St. Louis in 1958–59?

12) _____ Who, way back, signed a $65,000-a-year contract as a rookie player?

13) _____ Who was the first scoring champ to become a head coach?

14) _____ Who was the second?

15) _____ Who was the first player to average 30 points a game?

16) _____ Who grabbed 35 rebounds in the seventh game of the 1959–60 playoff finals?

17) _____ Who was the first cornerman to average 30 points a game?

18) _____ Which team was the first to boast of three players with 20-point averages?

19) _____ Who was the first NBA player to win a Rookie of the Year-MVP double?

20) _____ In 1960 Cincinnati, which drafted first, picked Oscar Robertson; and Los Angeles, which drafted second, chose Jerry West. New York, which drafted third, had to settle for whom?

35. COURT CHRONOLOGY X

Fill in the blanks.

1) _____ Who was the West Virginia coach who accompanied Jerry West to Los Angeles in the NBA?

2) _____ Who was the first guard to average 30 points a game?

3) _____ Who broke Bob Cousy's run of eight consecutive assist titles?

4) _____ Who broke Jack Twyman's points-per-game average as a forward?

5) _____ Who was the first center to lead the league in scoring and rebounding in the same year?

6) _____ Who was the first forward to lead the league in scoring and rebounding in the same year?

7) _____ What team was the first one added to the league since the merger of 1950?

8) _____ Whom did they draft first? He averaged 31.6 points a game.

9) _____ Who averaged over 50 points a game and scored more than 4,000 points in 1961–62?

10) _____ Who was the forward who averaged 38.3 points a game in a 48-game season that was shortened by military service?

11) _____ Whose basket gave Boston a 109–107 victory over Philadelphia in the seventh game of the 1961–62 Eastern Division finals?

12) _____ Who scored a record 61 points in a playoff game against Boston?

13) _____ Whose steal of a ball possessed by Bob Cousy resulted in a Laker playoff victory?

14) _____ Who was the Celtic teammate who beat out Bill Russell for Rookie of the Year laurels in 1956–57?

15) _____ Who was the first player to average ten-or-more assists a game in a season?

16) _____ Who was the league's leading scorer in 1962–63 who didn't make the All-Star Team?

17) _____ Between 1960–61 and 1965–66 Oscar Robertson led the league in assists every year except one (1962–63). Who paced the circuit that year?

18) _____ Oscar Robertson was "Mr. Outside" with Cincinnati. Who was "Mr. Inside?"

19) _____ Who was the coach who convinced Wilt Chamberlain to sacrifice offense for defense?

20) _____ Who was the first forward to average 20 rebounds a game?

36. COURT CHRONOLOGY XI

Fill in the blanks.

1) _____ Whose deflection of a Hal Greer inbound pass, with five seconds remaining in the Eastern Division finals between Philadelphia and Boston, preserved the Celtics' dynasty in 1964–65?

2) _____ Who became the first player to score a career total of 20,000 points?

3) _____ Who was the former Ohio State player who became the second forward to average 20 rebounds a game?

4) _____ Who was the first forward to average 20 rebounds a game for the second time?

5) _____ Who was the first $100,000-a-year player?

6) _____ Whom did another team pay $100,001 just to outdo the preceding player?

7) _____ What team won 45 of its first 49 games?

8) _____ Who was the former Piston and Bullet who succeeded Tommy Heinsohn upon his retirement?

9) _____ Who was the NBA's leading scorer who jumped to the ABA the following year?

10) _____ Who became the first guard to win the scoring title in 20 years?

11) _____ Who was his predecessor?

12) _____ Who was the rookie guard who finished fourth in scoring in 1967–68?

13) _____ Who was the Warrior big man who averaged over 20 rebounds a game in back-to-back years?

14) _____ Who was the Laker coach with whom Jerry West, Elgin Baylor, and Wilt Chamberlain first teamed up in Los Angeles?

15) _____ Who was the original league owner who bowed out of the pro game when he sold his Hawks to Atlanta?

16) _____ The acquisition of what cornerman turned the Knicks into league contenders in 1968–69?

17) _____ Whom did the Knicks trade for him? He was a player they at one time wanted to sign as their number-one draft choice.

18) _____ Who has been the smallest scoring champ in league history?

19) _____ Which team, in 1970–71, wiped out the Knicks' 19-game winning streak with a mark of 20 consecutive victories?

20) _____ What team, in 1972–73, posted an all-time low 9–73 record?

37. COURT CHRONOLOGY XII

Fill in the blanks.

1) _____ Who was the 6-8 center who led his team to the league championship in 1973–74?

2) _____ Who recorded a then record 910 assists in 1972–73?

3) _____ Whose league mark (908) did he break?

4) _____ Who became the Commissioner when Walter Kennedy retired?

5) _____ Who was the guard who scored 68 points in a 1976–77 game?

6) _____ What playoff runnerup lost 17 of its first 22 games during the regular season?

7) _____ Kareem Abdul-Jabbar broke his hand in a fight with what Milwaukee rookie?

8) _____ Who was sidelined for the remainder of the 1977–78 season as a result of a Kermit Washington right hand to the jaw?

9) _____ Who scored 73 points in a game on the last day of the season?

10) _____ Who was the league's leading scorer who ripped the nets for 63 points on the same day?

11) _____ Who was the first back-courtman to lead the league in scoring three straight years?

12) _____ Who has been the only Knick to lead the league in assist average for a season?

13) _____ When Calvin Murphy sank 95.7 percent of his free throws in 1980–81, he broke the former league record (94.7) of what former teammate?

14) _____ Which team, before the 1980–81 Nuggets, was the last team to boast of three 20-point scorers in the same year?

38. ALL-TIME GREATS I

Fill in the blanks.

1) _____ Who has won six MVP awards?

2) _____ Who was the player whose "off-balanced"

jump shot evened the 1968–69 championship series, against Los Angeles, at two games apiece?

3) _____ Who was the toughest defensive player that Bob Cousy, according to his own admission, played against?

4) _____ Who was the forward who averaged 26.4 points a game and 16.1 rebounds a contest in his 11-year career?

5) _____ Who averaged 27 points a game in a career during which he scored more points than any other guard except Oscar Robertson?

6) _____ Who has played on world championship teams in both Milwaukee and Los Angeles?

7) _____ Who was the first player ever to finish in the top five of four separate categories: scoring, rebounding, free throw percentage, and assists?

8) _____ Who retired as the third leading scorer and the fifth leading assistman in league history?

9) _____ Who was the forward who four times averaged better than 30 points a game, scored 64 points in a regular-season game and 55 points in a playoff game?

10) _____ Who quit college to join the Harlem Globetrotters while he waited for his class to graduate so that he could turn pro?

11) _____ Who broke into the league with a 30.5 scoring average and a 9.7 assist-per-game mark, the highest figure in that category that the league had yet seen?

12) _____ Who, when he finished his career in 1963–64, enjoyed the longest career (16 years) in league history? It's still the longest career.

13) _____ Who sank 56 consecutive foul shots in the playoffs?

14) _____ Who was the guard who led the league in game-scoring (34.9) and assists (11.4) in the same season?

15) _____ Who, when he retired, had more career points than any other player in league history, yet never led the league in season scoring?

16) _____ Who became the first guard since Slater

Martin, 20 years before, to lead the league in minutes played?

17) _____ Who was the NYU product who led the NBA in free throw percentage three times and ended up runnerup in that category on several occasions?

39. ALL-TIME GREATS II

Fill in the blanks.

1) _____ Who, during one stretch of his career, sank 79 of 80 foul tries?

2) _____ Who was the playmaker, other than Slater Martin, who fed Bob Pettit, Clyde Lovellette, and Cliff Hagan with the St. Louis Hawks?

3) _____ Who, in the seventh game of a championship series, scored 42 points, grabbed 13 rebounds, and fed off 12 assists for the losing club?

4) _____ Who was the first guard to average 22 points a game?

5) _____ Who was the outside shooter who set a Celtic season scoring record in 1964–65 when he netted 25.9 points a game?

6) _____ Who was the 6-5 swingman who led the Celtics in scoring, assists, and rebounds in the year that Bill Russell retired?

7) _____ Who was the pearl of a player who averaged 41.5 points a game and netted an NCAA record 1,329 points in his senior year at Winston-Salem College?

8) _____ Who was named the NBA's "Outstanding Player for the First 35 Years?"

9) _____ Who was the player-coach with both Seattle and Portland?

10) _____ Who registered more assists (7,211) than any other player except Oscar Robertson?

11) _____ Who, with a cast on his hand, scored 28 points and pulled down 26 rebounds in the 1958 All-Star Game?

12) _____ Who is the present-day star who was permanently suspended from his college team and denied an opportunity to play on the 1972 Olympic team because he punched an opposing player?

13) _____ Who, in 1969–70, was named the MVP in the All-Star Game, the regular season, and the playoffs?

14) _____ Who is the only man ever to coach winners in three major pro leagues?

15) _____ Who was the Celtic who averaged 45 minutes of playing time in both 1970–71 and 1971–72?

40. ALL-TIME GREATS III

Fill in the blanks.

1) _____ Who is the master of the sky hook?

2) _____ Who was the Philadelphia Warrior scoring champ who did not play high school basketball?

3) _____ Who is the great guard whom Bob Cousy coached at Kansas City–Omaha?

4) _____ Who has been the only player to lead the ABA and the NBA in scoring?

5) _____ Who handed off 21-or-more assists in a game 11 times?

6) _____ Who was the first center to lead the league in assists?

7) _____ Who was elected MVP of an All-Star Game after the award had already been given to another player?

8) _____ Who was the Boston Celtic who shared a Rookie of the Year Award with Geoff Petrie?

9) _____ Who, before Bobby Jones, was the 76ers' most effective sixth man?

10) _____ Who, in the last four years of his pro career, was named the All-Defensive Team's top vote-getter each year?

11) _____ Who was the one-time Rochester Royal who was the catalyst of the Seton Hall team that won 43 consecutive games in the early 1940s?

12) _____ What ABA player, more than any other, prompted the two-league merger?

13) _____ Who scored a season-high and record-high 43 points in the first BAA season?

14) _____ Who was the scoring champ that scout John Kerr found?

15) _____ Who was the Knick who, while a member of the 1967 Southern Illinois University five, won the MVP Award in the NIT?

41. ALL-TIME GREATS IV

Fill in the blanks.

1) _____ Who was the one-time Philadelphia player who, when he retired at the end of the 1972–73 season, held the NBA record for the most (1,122) games played?

2) _____ Who was the All-Pro great who was beaten out for wide receiver of the Cleveland Browns by another All-Pro, Gary Collins?

3) _____ Who was the All-Pro, from little North Carolina College, whom Wake Forest coach Bones McKinney recommended to Red Auerbach in 1957?

4) _____ Who, at the University of Texas, set the Southwest Conference scoring record of 49 points in a single game?

5) _____ Who was voted the "Greatest Basketball Player of the First Half Century?"

6) _____ Who scored a club record 56 points for Baltimore in his rookie year?

7) _____ Who placed no lower than fifth in the league as either a rebounder or scorer in his first ten years in the league?

8) _____ Who was the Knick who, moved from center to forward, made the second team on back-to-back All-Star teams?

9) _____ Who was the guard who scored 30 points a game in each of his first six years in the league?

10) _____ Who played on 11 championship clubs during a 13-year career?

11) _____ Who was the Syracuse Nat who led his team in foul shooting for 11 straight years?

12) _____ Who was the Celtic player who shut out Hal Greer in a playoff game?

13) _____ Who wrote an autobiography that was titled "Mr. Clutch?"

14) _____ Who won the MVP Award of the NIT when he led Providence to the finals in 1960?

15) _____ Who eight times blocked ten or more shots in a game?

42. ALL-TIME GREATS V

Fill in the blanks.

1) _____ Who, in 1958–59, shot a then-record 93.2 percent from the foul line?

2) _____ Who was the Celtic who played on a college team that won 55 consecutive games?

3) _____ Who was the "old pro" who, traded to Milwaukee in 1970–71, helped the Bucks win their first championship?

4) _____ Who was the big man who set a record for pivotmen when he scored 61 points in a game?

5) _____ Who was the Celtic guard who was an accomplished behind-the-back passer?

6) _____ Who was the Warrior back-courtman who was named to the NBA's second-team All-Star squad seven years in a row?

7) _____ Who was the one-time league scoring champion who died in a 1976 shooting incident?

8) _____ Who abandoned a major league baseball career when he was named the head coach of a pro basketball team?

9) _____ Who led the league in assists eight consecutive times?

10) _____ Who was the first player to reach the 10,000 point mark?

11) _____ Who had a record 40.6 point scoring average one year in the playoffs?

12) _____ Whose pro career was interrupted, after he had won a scoring title, by a two-year hitch in the Marine Corps?

13) _____ Who sank 60 consecutive free throws at the beginning of the 1976–77 season?

14) _____ Who was the one-time Knick who became the general manager of the New York Nets?

15) _____ Who is the scoring champ who, when he broke into the ABA, was a substitute on one of Julius Erving's teams?

43. ALL-TIME GREATS VI

Fill in the blanks.

1) _____ Who was the first black player to perform for a major college team (Marshall) in West Virginia?

2) _____ Who was the great playmaker of the great Minneapolis teams of the early 1950s?

3) _____ Who was the college player from the 1940s whom Ray Meyer converted into a great player?

4) _____ Who won or shared four MVP awards in All-Star play?

5) _____ Who set a record with 172 appearances in playoff games?

6) _____ Who was in the Dodger dugout when Bobby Thomson of the Giants hit his dramatic pennant-winning home run in 1951?

7) _____ Who is the coach who was the youngest to win his 400th game?

8) _____ Who was the Syracuse Nat who, by way of Fort Wayne and Detroit, capped off a brief-but-meritorious seven-year career by averaging 20.2 points per game during the (1959–60) season and 25.1 in the playoffs?

9) _____ Who averaged 20 points a game over the last 13 years of his 14-year career?

10) _____ Who, in the 1950s, led the league in free throw percentage seven times?

11) _____ Who was the Nat big man who made 3,000 assists, yet never led the league in that department?

12) _____ Who was the "Hawk" who averaged 25.5 points a game in 88 playoff get-togethers?

13) _____ Who was the floor general of championship teams in Minneapolis and St. Louis?

14) _____ Which fourth-year veteran took Bill Sharman's place after the veteran retired following the 1960–61 season?

15) _____ Who became the heir to Frank Ramsey as the Celtics' sixth man?

44. ALL-TIME GREATS VII

Fill in the blanks.

1) _____ Who was the Knick who, in the final game of the 1969–70 championship series, scored 36 points and handed off 19 assists?

2) _____ Who was the last commissioner of the ABA?

3) _____ Who was the center who averaged 24 points, 24 rebounds, and 8 assists a game in one season?

4) _____ Who was the one-time Warrior who once scored 85 points in one game for Villanova?

5) _____ Who has the highest career scoring average (29.1) in the playoffs?

6) _____ Whose arrival in Cincinnati prompted the Royals to trade Oscar Robertson to the Bucks?

7) _____ Who played on a pro team that was coached by Bruce Hale, his father-in-law who was his former coach at the University of Miami in Florida?

8) _____ Who scored 17 of his team's last 21 points in a playoff victory that was earned in four overtime periods?

9) _____ Who was the NBA player who, after he jumped to the ABA, was named MVP his first season in the "underling" league?

10) _____ Who pulled down a record 55 rebounds in one game?

11) _____ Who is the last player to win the NBA scoring title three straight years?

12) _____ Who was the 76er who copped the MVP Award of an All-Star game on the strength of eight-for-eight shooting from the floor?

13) _____ Who was the Celtic great who took more

career shots than any other player except Wilt Chamberlain?

14) Who, in an 11-year career, made the NBA First-Team All-Star squad ten times and the Second-Team in his final year?

15) _____ Who grabbed a record 4,104 rebounds in playoff competition?

45. ROOKIE YEARS: PART I

Joe Fulks, Dolph Schayes, and Carl Braun broke into big-league professional basketball in the seasons shown. Match the men with the correct seasons.

1) _____ (1946–47)
2) _____ (1947–48)
3) _____ (1948–49)

46. ROOKIE YEARS: PART II

Ralph Beard, Elgin Baylor, Bill Russell, Larry Costello, Woody Sauldsberry, Neil Johnston, Tom Gola, Bob Cousy, Jack McMahon, and Clyde Lovellette broke into the NBA in the seasons shown. Match the men with the correct seasons.

1) _____ (1949–50)   6) _____ (1954–55)
2) _____ (1950–51)   7) _____ (1955–56)
3) _____ (1951–52)   8) _____ (1956–57)
4) _____ (1952–53)   9) _____ (1957–58)
5) _____ (1953–54)   10) _____ (1958–59)

47. ROOKIE YEARS: PART III

Wilt Chamberlain, Elvin Hayes, Walt Bellamy, Jerry Lucas, John Havlicek, Happy Hairston, Rick Barry, Bill Bradley, Dave Bing, and Darrall Imhoff broke into the NBA in the seasons shown. Match the men with the correct seasons.

1) _____ (1959–60)   6) _____ (1964–65)
2) _____ (1960–61)   7) _____ (1965–66)
3) _____ (1961–62)   8) _____ (1966–67)
4) _____ (1962–63)   9) _____ (1967–68)
5) _____ (1963–64)   10) _____ (1968–69)

48. ROOKIE YEARS: PART IV

Kelly Tripucka, Bob Dandridge, Adrian Dantley, Jim Paxson, Moses Malone, Larry Smith, Doug Collins, Bernard King, George Gervin, Mychal Thompson, Nate Archibald, Darryl Dawkins, and Julius Erving broke into the NBA during the following seasons. Match the men with the correct seasons.

1) _____ (1969–70)   8) _____ (1976–77)
2) _____ (1970–71)   9) _____ (1977–78)
3) _____ (1971–72)   10) _____ (1978–79)
4) _____ (1972–73)   11) _____ (1979–80)
5) _____ (1973–74)   12) _____ (1980–81)
6) _____ (1974–75)   13) _____ (1981–82)
7) _____ (1975–76)

49. CAREER COUNTDOWN:
PART I

Nat Hickey, Harry Gallatin, Vern Mikkelsen, Frank Baumholtz, Fuzzy Levane, Bob Davies, Sid Tanenbaum, George Mikan, Alex Hannum, Ed Sadowski, George Senesky, Cliff Barker, and Alex Groza bowed out of big-league professional basketball during the following seasons. Match the men with the correct seasons.

1) _____ (1946–47) 8) _____ (1953–54)
2) _____ (1947–48) 9) _____ (1954–55)
3) _____ (1948–49) 10) _____ (1955–56)
4) _____ (1949–50) 11) _____ (1956–57)
5) _____ (1950–51) 12) _____ (1957–58)
6) _____ (1951–52) 13) _____ (1958–59)
7) _____ (1952–53)

50. CAREER COUNTDOWN:
PART II

Frank Ramsey, K.C. Jones, Wayne Embry, Dick McGuire, John Kerr, Larry Costello, Bill Sharman, Tom Heinsohn, Paul Arizin, and Dave Piontek bowed out of the NBA during the following seasons. Match the men with the correct seasons.

1) _____ (1959–60) 6) _____ (1964–65)
2) _____ (1960–61) 7) _____ (1965–66)
3) _____ (1961–62) 8) _____ (1966–67)
4) _____ (1962–63) 9) _____ (1967–68)
5) _____ (1963–64) 10) _____ (1968–69)

51. CAREER COUNTDOWN: PART III

Jo Jo White, Dave DeBusschere, Richie Guerin, Dave Cowens, Hal Greer, Fred Carter, Kevin Loughery, Gail Goodrich, Dave Stallworth, Bailey Howell, John Havlicek, and Billy Cunningham bowed out of the NBA during the following seasons. Match the men with the correct seasons.

1) _____ (1969–70)   7) _____ (1975–76)
2) _____ (1970–71)   8) _____ (1976–77)
3) _____ (1971–72)   9) _____ (1977–78)
4) _____ (1972–73)   10) _____ (1978–79)
5) _____ (1973–74)   11) _____ (1979–80)
6) _____ (1974–75)   12) _____ (1980–81)

52. SUB-20-POINT-A-GAME SCORERS

Mark a check opposite the names of the following retired players who never averaged 20 points a game during their pro careers.

John Green   Willie Wise
Joe Caldwell   Harry Gallatin
Mel Daniels   Dave DeBusschere
Bill Walton   Vern Mikkelsen
Wes Unseld   James Jones
Nate Thurmond   Tom Heinsohn
Dick Van Arsdale   Bill Bradley
Tom Van Arsdale   Bill Russell
Maurice Stokes   Larry Cannon

Lucius Allen
Kevin Loughery
Bob Davies
Tom Gola
Lou Hudson
Bailey Howell
Wayne Embry
Gus Johnson
Sam Jones
Jim Pollard
Carl Braun
Jerry Sloan
Jerry Lucas
Chet Walker
Happy Hairston
Max Zaslofsky

Fred Carter
Guy Rodgers
John Brisker
John Block
Frank Ramsey
Larry Foust
John Kerr
Louie Dampier
Terry Dischinger
Don Otten
Cliff Hagan
Jon McGlocklin
Jim McMillian
Geoff Petrie
Willis Reed
Walter Dukes

53. 800 ASSISTS

Six players have recorded 800-or-more assists in one season. How many of them can you name?

1) _____   4) _____
2) _____   5) _____
3) _____   6) _____

Flash Followup

1) _____ Who did it four times?

54. GOOD "D"

All of the players who are listed below made the all-league defensive team at least two times. Next to their names write "Yes" if they made it four times or more and "No" if they made it three times or less.

1) _____ Dave DeBusschere
2) _____ Nate Thurmond
3) _____ Walt Frazier
4) _____ Jerry Sloan
5) _____ Gus Johnson
6) _____ Jerry West
7) _____ John Havlicek
8) _____ Wilt Chamberlain
9) _____ Kareem Abdul-Jabbar
10) _____ Norm Van Lier
11) _____ Paul Silas
12) _____ Bobby Jones
13) _____ Bill Walton
14) _____ Don Buse
15) _____ Dennis Johnson
16) _____ Michael Ray Richardson

Flash Followup

1) _____ Which one of them made the team seven times?
2) _____ Who made it six times?

55. THREE-POINT SHOOTERS

In 1980–81 Mike Bratz led the NBA in three-point field goals with 57. The players who are listed below were good three-point shooters, too. If, in their best years, they scored more than 57 three-pointers, mark a check next to their names; there are 24 in all.

Henry Bibby
Larry Bird
Ron Boone
Fred Brown
Don Buse
Julius Erving
Chris Ford
George Gervin
Kevin Grevey
Joe Hassett
George McGinnis
Mike Newlin
John Roche
Brian Taylor
Freeman Williams
Brian Winters
Rick Barry
John Brisker
Roger Brown
Glen Courtney Combs
Jeff Congdon
Louie Dampier
Joe Hamilton
Art Heyman
Warren Jabali

Stewart Johnson
Rich Jones
Steve Jones
Larry Jones
Bill Keller
Wendell Ladner
Dwight Lamar
George Lehmann
Fred Lewis
Larry Miller
Rick Mount
Johnny Neumann
Jim Rayl
Les Selvage
Billy Shepherd
Alan Smith
Willie Somerset
George Stone
Skeeter Swift
George Thompson
Al Tucker
Chico Vaughn
Bob Verga
Ben Warley
Bob Warren

56. TWO-TEAM CHAMPS

There have not been too many players who have performed on two different championship teams. The players who are listed below are some of the exceptions. To get credit for the question, name both of the teams for which they suited up.

1) _____ Arnie Risen
2) _____ Slater Martin
3) _____ Clyde Lovellette
4) _____ Wilt Chamberlain
5) _____ Bob Dandridge
6) _____ Paul Silas
7) _____ Kareem Abdul-Jabbar

57. PROFILE OF A CHAMPION

In this quiz we're going to omit a forward, the center, a guard, and the coach of championship clubs down through the years. Insert the omitted forward on the first line, the center on the second line, the guard on the third line, and the coach on the fourth line. Sometimes two or more names are placed at a position, because they saw a similar amount of playing time. Some years are skipped over because the personnel on repeat teams remained virtually the same.

The 1946—47 Philadelphia Warriors

1) Joe Fulks   _____
2)   _____
3) _____   Angelo Musi
                   Jerry Fleishman
                   Ralph Kaplowitz
4) _____

The 1947—48 Baltimore Bullets

1) _____   Grady Lewis
2)   _____
3) Buddy Jeannette   _____
    Paul Hoffman
4) _____

The 1950–51 Rochester Royals

1) Jack Coleman   _____
2) _____   _____
3) _____   Bob Davies
                                   Red Holzman
4) _____

The 1951–52 Minneapolis Lakers

1) _____   Jim Pollard
2) _____   _____
3) Slater Martin   _____
   Pep Saul
4) _____

The 1954–55 Syracuse Nationals

1) Dolph Schayes   _____
2) _____   _____
3) _____   George King
4) _____

The 1955–56 Philadelphia Warriors

1) _____ or   Paul Arizin
   Walt Davis
2) _____   _____
3) Tom Gola   _____ or
                                   Ernie Beck or
                                   George Dempsey

4) _____

The 1956–57 Boston Celtics

1) Tom Heinsohn   _____
2)   _____
3) _____   Bob Cousy
4) _____

The 1957–58 St. Louis Hawks

1) _____   Bob Pettit
2)   _____
3) Slater Martin   _____
4) _____

The 1966–67 Philadelphia 76ers

1) _____   Chet Walker
                         Billy Cunningham
2)   _____
3) Hal Greer   _____ or
   Wally Jones   Bill Melchionni
4) _____

The 1968–69 Boston Celtics

1) _____ or   Don Nelson
   Satch Sanders
2)   _____
3) _____   John Havlicek
                         Larry Siegfried
4) _____

82

The 1969–70 New York Knicks

1) _____   Bill Bradley
2)   _____
3) Walt Frazier   _____
4) _____

The 1970–71 Milwaukee Bucks

1) Bob Dandridge   _____
2)   _____
3) _____   Jon McGlocklin
                                              Lucius Allen
4) _____

The 1971–72 Los Angeles Lakers

1) _____   Happy Hairston
2)   _____
3) Jerry West   _____
4) _____

The 1973–74 Boston Celtics

1) Don Nelson   _____
2)   _____
3) _____ or   John Havlicek
   Paul Westphal   Don Chaney
4) _____

The 1974-75 Golden State Warriors

1) ———   Rick Barry
2)   ———
3) Charles Johnson   ———
   Jeff Mullins
4) ———

The 1976-77 Portland Trail Blazers

1) Bob Gross   ———
2)   ———
3) ———   Johnny Davis
                                  Larry Steele
4) ———

The 1977-78 Washington Bullets

1) ———   Elvin Hayes
2)   ———
3) Larry Wright   ———
   Charley Johnson
4) ———

The 1978-79 Seattle SuperSonics

1) John Johnson   ———
2)   ———
3) ———   Gus Williams
4) ———

The 1979-80 Los Angeles Lakers

1) _____ or   Jamaal Wilkes
   Spencer Haywood
2)   _____
3) Magic Johnson   _____
4) _____

The 1980-81 Boston Celtics

1) Larry Bird   _____
2)   _____
3) _____ .   Chris Ford
                        M. L. Carr
4) _____

58. HALL OF FAMERS

Mark a check next to the names of the players listed
below who are in the Hall of Fame. There should be 21.

Jerry West   Sam Jones
Jerry Lucas   Hal Greer
Willis Reed   Bailey Howell
Paul Arizin   Elgin Baylor
Neil Johnston   Wilt Chamberlain
Joe Fulks   Nate Thurmond
Slater Martin   Walt Bellamy
Tom Heinsohn   Bob Cousy
Dolph Schayes   Gail Goodrich

Bill Sharman   Cliff Hagan
Jack Twyman   Tom Gola
Bob Pettit   Clyde Lovellette
Bob Davies   Frank Ramsey
George Yardley   Dave DeBusschere
Walt Frazier   Andy Phillip
George Mikan   Guy Rodgers
Jim Pollard   Bill Russell
Ed Macauley   Oscar Robertson
Max Zaslofsky   Bones McKinney

59. THE HALL OF FAME

1) _____ Who was the two-time scoring champ who retired (1962) as the third highest scorer (16,266) in NBA history? He played in ten All-Star games—he was the MVP in 1952—and he scored more than 20 points a game in his last nine seasons.

2) _____ The winningest NBA coach of all time (938), he led clubs to nine divisional titles and eight straight world championships. Who is he?

3) _____ Who was the forward who averaged 27.4 points a game during a 14-year career and scored 23,149 career points, the fifth highest figure in NBA history? A Rookie of the Year selection and All-Star Game MVP, he once scored 71 points in a regular-season game.

4) _____ Who was the Boston Celtic organizer who was one of the founding fathers of the game?

5) _____ Who was the four-time MVP winner who played 47,859 minutes without once fouling out of a game? He played for championship teams on both the East and West Coast.

6) _____ Who was the number-three all-time assist-maker (6,959) who made the All-NBA First Team ten

years in a row and played on championship teams in six of his last seven years in the league? He scored 16,960 career points, an average of 18.4 per game.

7) _____ Who was the popular floorman who was All-League seven times in a ten-year career in which he led the Royals to three titles?

8) _____ Who was the Warrior jump shooter who hit 49 consecutive free throws on two different occasions? A league scoring champion, he averaged better than 20 points a game his first three years in the league.

9) _____ Who was the Warrior back-courtman who became the second player to win All-American honors all four years that he was in college? He was named the MVP in the 1952 NIT and the 1954 NCAA.

10) _____ Who was one of the organizers of the NBA who coached the Philadelphia Sphas in 1918 and the Philadelphia Warriors in 1955? He later served as a club owner, league consultant, and schedule maker.

11) _____ Who was the one-time Hawk shooter who was a key player for St. Louis, which won six divisional titles and the NBA crown in 1957–58? He averaged 18.5 points per game during a ten-year career that was highlighted by an MVP award.

12) _____ Who was the club owner who coached his team to an NBL title in 1946 and an NBA crown in 1951? He served as a member of the Board of Directors of the NBL, the BAA, and the NBA.

13) _____ Who introduced the basketball doubleheader to Madison Square Garden in 1934 and founded the New York Knicks in 1946?

14) _____ Who was the referee, the game's most famous, who attracted fans with his colorful performances?

15) _____ Who was the BAA's public relations director who served as the NBA Commissioner from 1963–75?

16) _____ Who was the 1964 Rookie of the Year and the 1965 MVP who scored 14,053 career points and pulled down 12,942 rebounds in an 11-year career with the Royals, the Warriors, and the Knicks? At the time of his election, he was the league's sixth leading all-time

rebounder. Twice he averaged 20 rebounds a game during a season.

17) _____ Who was the St. Louis-Boston center—he once scored 46 points against George Mikan—who became the youngest player (32) to be elected to the Hall of Fame?

18) _____ Who was the Player of the Year (1944–45 and 1945–46) in college and the Player of the First Half Century in pro basketball?

19) _____ Who was the Rookie of the Year, the All-Star MVP (four times), and the league MVP (twice) who retired from the game as the league's all-time scorer?

20) _____ Who was the back-courtman for the Stags, the Warriors, the Pistons, and the Celtics who was once the leader of the famed "Whiz Kids" of the University of Illinois? He was the leader in assists two times and the runnerup four times.

21) _____ Who was the man with a strong legal and administrative background who served as the Commissioner for 17 years?

22) _____ Who was the small forward who complemented George Mikan as the Lakers won two NBL titles and four NBA crowns during pro basketball's first dynasty?

23) _____ Who was the Rookie of the Year (1961), the MVP (1964), and the All-Star Game MVP (1961, 1964, and 1969) who scored more points (26,710) than any other guard, fed off more assists (9,887) than any other player, and sank more foul shots (7,694) than any other player?

24) _____ Who was the five-time MVP who player-coached a team to two world titles?

25) _____ Who was the 12-time member of the All-Star team who set records for career scoring and career games before he retired in 1963–64? His son is a present-day player in the NBA.

26) _____ Who was the All-NBA guard of seven years who retired with a free throw mark of 89 percent? He has been the only player to coach winners in three different leagues: Cleveland Pipers (ABL), Utah Jazz (ABA), and Los Angeles Lakers (NBA)?

27) _____ Who was the 27-point-per-game guard who scored a record 4,457 points in playoff competition?

28) _____ Who was the "sixth man" who was elected to the Hall of Fame in 1982?

29) _____ Who began his pro career with the 1949–50 Lakers, who won the NBA title, and concluded his career with the 1959–60 Hawks, who lost to Boston in seven games in the championship series?

30) _____ Who was the Knick, a Rookie of the Year in 1965, and an MVP in 1970, who was elected to the Hall of Fame in 1982?

31) _____ Who was the former Nat-Sixer, the eighth leading scorer of all time, who gained entrance in 1982?

60. FULL-COURT PRESS

1) _____ Who has led the NBA in assists four times?

2) _____ Who blocked a record 17 shots in one game?

3) _____ Who is the present-day player who shot a record .786 (11 for 14) in an All-Star game?

4) _____ Who is the present-day player who has led both the ABA and NBA in three-point field goal percentage?

5) _____ Who is the present-day back-courtman who has been named the MVP in the ABA All-Star Game and the NBA All-Star Game?

6) _____ Who was the three-time scoring champ who once pitched in the Phillie organization?

7) _____ Who was the Celtic back-courtman who played on ten championship clubs?

8) _____ Who is the former Ohio State standout who has been one of only seven players to average 20 points and 20 rebounds during his NCAA career?

9) _____ Who is the former Knick who was a playoff MVP winner twice?

10) _____ Who is the former back-court star who was named the MVP in three NBA All-Star games?

11) _____ Who is the retired player who is the all-time playoff leader in both rebounds and personal fouls?

12) _____ Who is the former minor league baseball player who was named the Coach of the Year in both the ABA and the NBA?

13) _____ Who is the former player who holds the one-year NCAA field goal percentage high (76.3) and the career high (68.6)?

14) _____ Who is the former West Coast star who shares the one-game playoff record in assists with 19?

15) _____ Who is the former East Coast guard who also shares the above record?

16) _____ Who scored 21 points in one quarter of an NBA championship game? He played with the Warriors.

17) _____ Who once scored a record 19 points in one quarter of an All-Star game?

18) _____ Who is the former Celtic who once scored a record nine points in overtime?

19) _____ Who has been named the regular-season MVP six times?

20) _____ Who set ABA season and career records for most free throws attempted and most free throws made?

21) _____ Who is the present-day player who has been named the MVP in both the ABA and the NBA and is the former U-Mass player who averaged over 20 points and 20 rebounds during his NCAA career?

22) _____ Who is the present-day player who once scored a record 33 points in one quarter?

23) _____ Who is the present-day player who, while in the ABA, won Rookie of the Year and MVP honors in the same year?

24) _____ Who holds the ABA record for most points in one season?

25) _____ Who is the Sixer boardman who shares the ABA record for most shots (12) blocked in one game?

26) _____ Who is the Sixer who led both the ABA and the NBA in field goal percentage?

27) _____ Who was the playoff MVP in 1981?

28) _____ Who is the West Coast boardman who has led both the ABA and NBA in season rebounding?

29) _____ Who is the present-day player who once scored a record 13 field goals in one quarter.

30) _____ Who is the retired player who once pulled down 40 rebounds in a championship series game?

61. NAME THAT TEAM

In this quiz you'll be given the cities in which the 23 NBA franchises reside. All you have to do is to give the names of the respective teams.

1) Oakland	_____	13) Boston	_____
2) Los Angeles	_____	14) New Jersey	_____
3) Phoenix	_____	15) New York	_____
4) Portland	_____	16) Philadelphia	_____
5) San Diego	_____	17) Washington	_____
6) Seattle	_____	18) Atlanta	_____
7) Dallas	_____	19) Chicago	_____
8) Denver	_____	20) Cleveland	_____
9) Houston	_____	21) Detroit	_____
10) Kansas City	_____	22) Indiana	_____
11) San Antonio	_____	23) Milwaukee	_____
12) Utah	_____		

62. CONFERENCE AND DIVISION PLAY

Place the following teams in their respective conferences and divisions: New Jersey Nets, Seattle SuperSonics, Detroit Pistons, Dallas Mavericks, Milwaukee Bucks, San Antonio Spurs, Boston Celtics, Phoenix Suns, San Diego Clippers, Washington Bullets, Cleveland Cavaliers, Utah Jazz, Philadelphia 76ers, Kansas City Kings, Los Angeles Lakers, Chicago Bulls, New York Knicks, Portland Trail Blazers, Indiana Pacers, Houston Rockets, Atlanta Hawks, Golden State Warriors, and Denver Nuggets. Any order of placement within the respective divisions is acceptable.

Eastern Conference

Atlantic Division

1) ———
2) ———
3) ———
4) ———
5) ———

Central Division

6) ———
7) ———
8) ———
9) ———
10) ———
11) ———

Western Conference

Midwest Division

12) ———
13) ———
14) ———
15) ———
16) ———
17) ———

Pacific Division

18) ———
19) ———
20) ———
21) ———
22) ———
23) ———

63. CHAMPIONSHIP CLUBS

You are going to be presented with the Eastern Division and the Western Division winners since the 1946–47 season. In many instances one of those two winners copped the playoff championship, also. But in some cases a dark-horse playoff entry emerged as the league champion. Can you identify the NBA champions from the stated or suggested clues?

Season	Champion	Eastern Division	Western Division
1) 1946–47	_____	Washington	Chicago
2) 1947–48	_____	Philadelphia	St. Louis
3) 1948–49	_____	Washington	Rochester
4) 1949–50	_____	Syracuse	Indianapolis
5) 1950–51	_____	Philadelphia	Minneapolis
6) 1951–52	_____	Syracuse	Rochester
7) 1952–53	_____	New York	Minneapolis
8) 1953–54	_____	New York	Minneapolis
9) 1954–55	_____	Syracuse	Fort Wayne
10) 1955–56	_____	Philadelphia	Fort Wayne
11) 1956–57	_____	Boston	St. Louis
12) 1957–58	_____	Boston	St. Louis
13) 1958–59	_____	Boston	St. Louis
14) 1959–60	_____	Boston	St. Louis
15) 1960–61	_____	Boston	St. Louis
16) 1961–62	_____	Boston	Los Angeles
17) 1962–63	_____	Boston	Los Angeles
18) 1963–64	_____	Boston	San Francisco
19) 1964–65	_____	Boston	Los Angeles
20) 1965–66	_____	Philadelphia	Los Angeles
21) 1966–67	_____	Philadelphia	San Francisco
22) 1967–68	_____	Philadelphia	St. Louis

23)	1968–69 _____	Baltimore	Los Angeles
24)	1969–70 _____	New York	Atlanta
25)	1970–71 _____	Baltimore	Milwaukee
26)	1971–72 _____	New York	Los Angeles
27)	1972–73 _____	New York	Los Angeles
28)	1973–74 _____	Boston	Milwaukee
29)	1974–75 _____	Washington	Golden State
30)	1975–76 _____	Boston	Phoenix
31)	1976–77 _____	Philadelphia	Portland
32)	1977–78 _____	Washington	Seattle
33)	1978–79 _____	Washington	Seattle
34)	1979–80 _____	Boston	Los Angeles
35)	1980–81 _____	Boston	Phoenix
36)	1981–82 _____	Philadelphia	Los Angeles

64. ONCE UPON A TIME

Once upon a time, the cities, states, and places in the left-hand column below had professional franchises. Can you match the teams and their dates with their corresponding names in the right-hand column? The teams are to be considered NBA clubs, unless otherwise noted.

1)	__ Anaheim (ABA)	(1967–68)	a)	Oaks
2)	__ Anderson	(1949–50)	b)	Huskies
3)	__ Buffalo	(1970–78)	c)	Hawks
4)	__ Carolina (ABA)	(1969–73)	d)	Braves
5)	__ Fort Wayne	(1948–57)	e)	Amigos
6)	__ Kentucky	(1967–76)	f)	Redskins
7)	__ Miami (ABA)	(1968–72)	g)	Colonels
8)	__ Oakland (ABA)	(1967–69)	h)	Nationals
9)	__ Providence	(1946–49)	i)	Packers
10)	__ Sheboygan	(1949–50)	j)	Squires
11)	__ Syracuse	(1947–63)	k)	Cougars

12) ___ Texas (ABA)	(1970–71)	l) Steamrollers
13) ___ Toronto	(1946–47)	m) Pistons
14) ___ Tri-Cities	(1949–51)	n) Floridians
15) ___ Virginia (ABA)	(1970–76)	o) Blackhawks
16) ___ Waterloo	(1949–50)	p) Chaparrals

65. SETTING THE RECORD STRAIGHT

Each of the professional basketball teams since 1946 is listed below. Their records, in correct or inverted form, are placed beside them. If you believe the record, as printed, is correct, write a "C" next to it; if you believe it is incorrect, write an "I." The records are conclusive through the 1981 season.

1) Anaheim Amigos	25	53	___
2) Anderson Packers	37	27	___
3) Tri-Cities Black Hawks	78	54	___
4) Milwaukee Hawks	190	91	___
5) St. Louis Hawks	533	456	___
6) Atlanta Hawks	508	568	___
7) Baltimore Bullets	303	161	___
8) Boston Celtics	1646	1011	___
9) Buffalo Braves	262	394	___
10) Capital Bullets	37	45	___
11) Carolina Cougars	168	168	___
12) Chicago Bulls	621	608	___
13) Chicago Packers	18	62	___
14) Chicago Stags	92	145	___
15) Chicago Zephyrs	25	55	___
16) Cincinnati Royals	582	535	___
17) Cleveland Cavaliers	369	533	___
18) Cleveland Rebels	30	30	___

19)	Dallas Chapparrals	108	132	——
20)	Dallas Mavericks	15	67	——
21)	Denver Rockets	288	288	——
22)	Denver Nuggets	11	51	——
23)	Denver Nuggets (ABA-NBA)	241	337	——
24)	Detroit Falcons	40	20	——
25)	Fort Wayne Pistons	326	313	——
26)	Detroit Pistons	793	1114	——
27)	Philadelphia Warriors	568	545	——
28)	Golden State Warriors	779	759	——
29)	Houston Mavericks	52	104	——
30)	Houston Rockets	327	435	——
31)	Indiana Pacers	613	541	——
32)	Indianapolis Jets	18	42	——
33)	Indianapolis Olympians	137	132	——
34)	Rochester Royals	357	263	——
35)	Kansas City Kings	440	420	——
36)	Kentucky Colonels	448	296	——
37)	Minneapolis Lakers	457	382	——
38)	Los Angeles Lakers	1021	687	——
39)	Los Angeles Stars	86	76	——
40)	Memphis Pros	67	101	——
41)	New Orleans Buccaneers	136	104	——
42)	Memphis Tams	45	123	——
43)	Memphis Sounds	57	27	——
44)	Minnesota Muskies	50	28	——
45)	Miami Floridians	191	139	——
46)	Milwaukee Bucks	628	438	——
47)	Minnesota Pipers	42	36	——
48)	New Jersey Americans	42	36	——
49)	New Jersey Nets	597	467	——
50)	New Orleans Jazz	161	249	——
51)	New York Knicks	1340	1313	——
52)	Oakland Oaks	82	74	——
53)	Syracuse Nats	576	437	——
54)	Philadelphia 76ers	820	649	——
55)	Phoenix Suns	527	539	——
56)	Pittsburgh Pipers	79	83	——
57)	Pittsburgh Condors	61	107	——

58)	Pittsburgh Ironmen	15	45	—
59)	Portland Trail Blazers	497	405	—
60)	Providence Steamrollers	46	122	—
61)	St. Louis Bombers	125	122	—
62)	St. Louis Spirits	114	138	—
63)	San Antonio Spurs	279	387	—
64)	San Diego Clippers	132	124	—
65)	San Diego Conquistadors	98	154	—
66)	San Diego Rockets	119	209	—
67)	San Diego Sails	8	3	—
68)	Seattle SuperSonics	597	551	—
69)	Sheboygan Redskins	40	22	—
70)	Toronto Huskies	38	22	—
71)	Utah Jazz	112	52	—
72)	Utah Stars	265	171	—
73)	Washington Capitols (ABA)	44	40	—
74)	Virginia Squires	303	200	—
75)	Baltimore Bullets	411	402	—
76)	Washington Bullets	332	242	—
77)	Washington Capitols	157	114	—
78)	Waterloo Hawks	43	19	—

66. RECORD (TEAM) REVIEW

1) _____ What team won an all-time high 69 games in one season?

2) _____ What team won an all-time low nines game in one season?

3) _____ What team, in addition to the 76ers, won 37 games at home? Both teams have actually performed the feat twice.

4) _____ What team lost 33 games at home?

5) _____ What team won 32 games on the road?

6) _____ What team, in addition to the 1974–75 Jazz, lost 38 games on the road?

7) _____ What team won a six-overtime-period game?

8) _____ What team lost the above game?

9) _____ What team won 33 games in a row?

10) _____ What team won 15 straight games at the start of the season?

11) _____ What team won 36 consecutive games at home?

12) _____ What team lost 20 consecutive games at home?

13) _____ What team won seven consecutive games in the playoffs?

14) _____ What team scored the most (10,143) points in a season?

15) _____ What team allowed the most (10,261) points in a season?

16) _____ What team had a .529 percent shooting average for the season?

17) _____ What team had an .821 mark from the free throw line for the year?

18) _____ What team pulled down the most (6,131) rebounds?

19) _____ What team dished out the most (2,562) assists?

20) _____ What team scored 100 points in 81 of its 82 games?

21) _____ What team had the most players (6) who scored 1,000 points in a season?

22) _____ What team scored 173 points in one game?

23) _____ What team scored 24 consecutive points?

67. PRO DEBUTS

With what teams did the retired players who are listed below debut in the NBA?

1) Lucius Allen _____
2) Dick Barnett _____
3) Larry Costello _____
4) Dave DeBusschere _____
5) Larry Foust _____
6) Gail Goodrich _____
7) Hal Green _____
8) Connie Hawkins _____
9) Spencer Haywood _____
10) Butch Komives _____
11) Rudy LaRusso _____
12) Kevin Loughery _____
13) Bob Love _____
14) Ed Macauley _____
15) Pete Maravich _____
16) George Mikan _____
17) Bob Pettit _____
18) Andy Phillip _____
19) Arnie Risen _____
20) Cazzie Russell _____
21) Bill Sharman _____
22) Gene Shue _____
23) Paul Silas _____
24) Jerry Sloan _____
25) Chet Walker _____

68. BREAKING IN

With what teams did the present-day players who are listed below break into the ABA?

1) Nate Archibald _____
2) Dennis Awtrey _____
3) Henry Bibby _____
4) Harvey Catchings _____
5) Adrian Dantley _____
6) Alex English _____
7) Lloyd Free _____
8) George Gervin _____
9) Elvin Hayes _____
10) Lionel Hollins _____
11) Mickey Johnson _____
12) Dwight Jones _____
13) Larry Kenon _____
14) Bob Lanier _____
15) Moses Malone _____
16) Steve Mix _____
17) Calvin Murphy _____
18) Kevin Porter _____
19) James Silas _____
20) Ricky Sobers _____
21) Brian Taylor _____
22) Foots Walker _____
23) Marvin Webster _____
24) Paul Westphal _____
25) Sidney Wicks _____

69. BOWING OUT

With what teams did the retired players who are listed below bow out of the NBA?

1) Rick Barry _____
2) Zelmo Beaty _____
3) Dave Bing _____
4) Fred Carter _____
5) Bob Cousy _____
6) Larry Foust _____
7) Gail Goodrich _____
8) Richie Guerin _____
9) Cliff Hagan _____
10) Bailey Howell _____
11) John Kerr _____
12) Rudy LaRusso _____
13) Clyde Lovellette _____
14) Slater Martin _____
15) Dick McGuire _____
16) Al McGuire _____
17) Tom Meschery _____
18) Willie Naulls _____
19) Don Ohl _____
20) Andy Phillip _____
21) Guy Rodgers _____
22) Cazzie Russell _____
23) Nate Thurmond _____
24) Jo Jo White _____
25) Max Zaslofsky _____

70. THE TRAILBLAZERS

Three of the most powerful teams of early professional basketball were the Original Celtics, the New York Rens, and the Buffalo Germans. From each of the lines below, one of the three players listed performed for each team. Place their names under the appropriate team names.

Pete Barry	Clarence Jenkins	Al Heerdt
William Rhode	Bill Yancey	Dutch Dehnert
Casey Holt	George Redlein	Nat Holman
Pappy Ricks	Johnny Beckman	Alfred Manweiler
Joe Lapchick	Ed Miller	Eyre Saitch
Hank Faust	Davey Banks	Willie Smith
Tarzan Cooper	Ernie Reich	Ed Reimann

The Celtics   The Rens   The Germans

1) ———   1) ———   1) ———
2) ———   2) ———   2) ———
3) ———   3) ———   3) ———
4) ———   4) ———   4) ———
5) ———   5) ———   5) ———
6) ———   6) ———   6) ———
7) ———   7) ———   7) ———

71. HIGH PERCENTAGE WINNERS

Name four teams with winning percentages above .800 that have won league championships.

1) ———— 3) ————
2) ———— 4) ————

72. HIGH-PERCENTAGE SECOND-PLACE FINISHERS

Four teams with winning percentages of .720-or-above have finished second. (One of them did it twice.) How many of them can you name?

1) ———— 3) ————
2) ———— 4) ————

73. LOW PERCENTAGE WINNERS

Name the three teams with winning percentages below .500 that have copped division championships.

1) ———— 3) ————
2) ————

74. TEAM MAGNATES

Match the NBA owners and presidents with the teams that they guide(d).

1) __ Walter Brown
2) __ Ned Irish
3) __ Max Winter

4) __ Danny Biasone
5) __ Eddie Gottlieb
6) __ Jack Kent Cooke
7) __ Frank Mieuli
8) __ Fred Zollner
9) __ Ben Kerner
10) __ Wes Pavalon

a) (Minneapolis) Lakers
b) Warriors
c) (San Francisco) Warriors
d) (Los Angeles) Lakers
e) (St. Louis) Hawks
f) Celtics
g) (Milwaukee) Bucks
h) Nats
i) Pistons
j) Knicks

75. TEAM COLORS

Match the uniform colors that are listed below with the teams that wear them. Seven teams in the league wear red, white, and blue.

Red, White, and Gold
Green and White
Red, White, and Blue
Wine and Gold
Blue and Green
Red and Gold
Blue and Gold

Royal Purple and Gold
Forest Green, Red, and White
Purple, Orange, and Copper
Scarlet, Black, and White
Metallic Silver and Black
Green and Gold
Purple, Green, and Gold

1) _____ Lakers		11) _____ SuperSonics	
2) _____ Pistons		12) _____ 76ers	
3) _____ Celtics		13) _____ Trail Blazers	
4) _____ Knicks		14) _____ Jazz	
5) _____ Bullets		15) _____ Spurs	
6) _____ Hawks		16) _____ Cavaliers	
7) _____ Mavericks		17) _____ Suns	
8) _____ Kings		18) _____ Nets	
9) _____ Bulls		19) _____ Rockets	
10) _____ Bucks		20) _____ Pacers	

76. RETIRED NUMBERS

We'll provide the teams that have retired uniform numbers, the number of numbers they have retired, and the numbers they have retired. Let's see if you can name the players who wore them.

Atlanta
1) _____ (9)
2) _____ (23)

Boston
1) _____ (1)
2) _____ (6)
3) _____ (10)
4) _____ (14)
5) _____ (15)
6) _____ (16)
7) _____ (17)
8) _____ (18)
9) _____ (19)
10) _____ (21)
11) _____ (22)
12) _____ (23)
13) _____ (24)
14) _____ (25)

Chicago	1) _____	(4)
Cleveland	1) _____	(7)
	2) _____	(34)
	3) _____	(42)
Denver	4) _____	(40)
Golden State	1) _____	(14)
	2) _____	(16)
	3) _____	(42)
Kansas City	1) _____	(12)
	2) _____	(14)
	3) _____	(27)
Los Angeles	1) _____	(22)
Milwaukee	1) _____	(1)
	2) _____	(14)
New Jersey	1) _____	(4)
	2) _____	(25)
New York	1) _____	(10)
	2) _____	(19)
	3) _____	(22)
Philadelphia	1) _____	(15)
	2) _____	(32)
Phoenix	1) _____	(5)
	2) _____	(42)
Portland	1) _____	(13)
	2) _____	(15)
	3) _____	(36)
	4) _____	(45)
Seattle	1) _____	(19)
Washington	1) _____	(41)

* As we were going to press, some teams were planning to retire the uniform numbers of additional players.

HAVLICEK STOLE THE BALL

The last minutes of the 1969 Eastern Conference play-off final are some of the most memorable sixty seconds in professional post-season history.

With host Boston and Philadelphia tied at three games—each team had won on the home court—the Celtics led the 76ers 110–103 with three minutes remaining in the game. But Wilt Chamberlain, whom the Sixers had reacquired from the San Francisco Warriors in midseason, scored on a tap-in and two free throws to whittle the gap to three points with just 31 seconds to go.

The Celtic lead seemed insurmountable, however, as Sam Jones went into a one-man stall. But Jones, after a fantastic dribbling display, made one of the most critical mistakes of his celebrated career. He held the ball too long and lost it via a 24-second violation. Philadelphia quickly capitalized on the turnover as Chamberlain stuffed a two-pointer to cut the lead to one with just five seconds left on the clock.

The Celtic lead still seemed safe. All Coach Red Auerbach's players had to do was to pass the ball inbounds, hold it, and head for Los Angeles and the playoff finals. But Bill Russell's inbounds pass hit the guide wire, and the Sixers got still one more life. Now Philadelphia, which had the ball underneath its own basket, seemed to be in control. Chamberlain, a future Hall-of-Famer, posted low; and another future Hall-of-Famer got set to pass the ball to him. But Russell checked Chamberlain closely, and the passer was forced to go deep to Chet Walker.

Out of nowhere, according to the player who committed the turnover, John Havlicek raced across the court, leaped, and deflected the ball to Sam Jones, who finally ran out the clock as Celtic announcer Johnny Most screamed into his mike: "Havlicek stole the ball. He stole the ball. He stole the ball. The Celtics win. Havlicek stole the ball."

From whom did Havlicek steal the ball? Here's another hint: The player who passed the ball finally got the big assist in 1982 when he was inducted into the Hall of Fame.

Answer: Hal Greer

SECOND-PERIOD SCORE

(Total just the second-period points.)

Points
You __ The NBA __
Games
You __ The NBA __

THE THIRD QUARTER

77. SCORING CHAMPIONS

Eighteen players have won scoring titles in the NBA. Match them up with the teams listed below. One won titles with two different teams.

1) _____ Philadelphia
2) _____ Philadelphia
3) _____ Philadelphia
4) _____ Philadelphia
5) _____ Detroit
6) _____ Detroit
7) _____ San Francisco
8) _____ San Francisco
9) _____ Chicago
10) _____ Minneapolis
11) _____ St. Louis
12) _____ San Diego
13) _____ Los Angeles
14) _____ Buffalo
15) _____ Kansas City-Omaha
16) _____ New Orleans
17) _____ San Antonio
18) _____ Utah

78. ONCE IS NOT ENOUGH

Eight of the players in the preceding quiz won the scoring title more than once. Match them up with the number of times that they did it.

1) _____ (7)   5) _____ (3)
2) _____ (3)   6) _____ (2)
3) _____ (3)   7) _____ (2)
4) _____ (3)   8) _____ (2)

79. THEY MADE THEIR POINT

Going into the 1981–82 season, Bob Pettit ranked tenth on the all-time list of career scorers. He scored 20,880 points. That's not too shabby for a guy who played only 11 professional seasons. But nine players—all but two of them retired—netted more points. How many of them can you name?

1) _____   6) _____
2) _____   7) _____
3) _____   8) _____
4) _____   9) _____
5) _____

Flash Followup

1) _____ Who was the only player to score more than 30,000 points? Actually, for the record, he scored 31,419.

80. SUPER SCORERS

Nine players—all except one of them retired—have scored 61 or more points in a game. How many of them can you name?

1) ———   6) ———
2) ———   7) ———
3) ———   8) ———
4) ———   9) ———
5) ———

Flash Followup

1) ——— Who scored an all-time high 100 points in one game?

81. FIELD GOAL MARKSMEN

At the end of the 1980–81 season, only one retired player was a member of the all-time top-ten field goal percentage shooters. How many of the nine current players who are on that list can you name?

1) _____   6) _____
2) _____   7) _____
3) _____   8) _____
4) _____   9) _____
5) _____

Flash Followup

1) _____ Who is the retired player who is on the list?

82. THE BOARDMEN

Paul Silas, at the end of the 1980–81 season, ranked tenth on the all-time list of rebounders. How many of the top nine—all but one of them retired—can you name?

1) _____   6) _____
2) _____   7) _____
3) _____   8) _____
4) _____   9) _____
5) _____

Flash Followup

1) _____ Who ranked first with the unbelievable total of 23,924 rebounds?

83. THEY COULDN'T RESIST THE ASSIST

At the end of the 1980–81 season, Norm Van Lier ranked tenth on the all-time list of assistmen. He had 5,217. Who were the nine players, all but two of them retired, who preceded his name on that select list?

1) _____   6) _____
2) _____   7) _____
3) _____   8) _____
4) _____   9) _____
5) _____

Flash Followup

1) _____ Who tops the list with an incredible total of 9,887?

84. .900-PLUS FREE-THROW SHOOTERS

Match the following players with their highest free throw percentage: Bobby Wanzer, Bill Sharman, Dolph

Schayes, Adrian Smith, Rick Barry, Ernie Di Gregorio, Calvin Murphy, and Ricky Sobers.

1) _____ .958   5) _____ .932
2) _____ .947   6) _____ .904
3) _____ .945   7) _____ .904
4) _____ .935   8) _____ .903

85. THEY WERE FINE ON THE LINE

At the end of the 1980–81 season, there were ten players—all of them retired—who had sunk more than 5,000 free throws. Chet Walker (5,079) was tenth on that all-time list. Who were the first nine?

1) _____   6) _____
2) _____   7) _____
3) _____   8) _____
4) _____   9) _____
5) _____

Flash Followup

1) _____ Who is the player who sank an all-time high 7,694 foul shots?

86. FREE THROW MARKSMEN

Dolph Schayes ranks tenth on the all-time list of free throw shooters. He had a mark of .844. How many of the nine players who rank ahead of him can you name? Six of them are still playing. (Records are conclusive through the 1980–81 season.)

1) ————   6) ————
2) ————   7) ————
3) ————   8) ————
4) ————   9) ————
5) ————

Flash Followup

1) ———— Who is the retired player who heads the list with a mark of .900?

87. 43-MINUTE GAMES

Going into the 1981–82 season, eight players had ticked off 3,500 or more minutes of play in a season. That breaks down to an average of approximately 43 minutes a game for an 82-contest season. How many of them can you name?

1) _____   5) _____
2) _____   6) _____
3) _____   7) _____
4) _____   8) _____

Flash Followup

Who are the two who performed the durable feat four times each?

1) _____   2) _____

88. MOST MINUTES

There are five players who have amassed more than 40,000 minutes of playing time during their careers. How many of them can you name?

1) _____   4) _____
2) _____   5) _____
3) _____

Flash Followup

1) _____ Who played the most (47,859) minutes?

89. FAIR OR FOUL

Frank Ramsey was one of the best sixth men who ever played the game. Yet, he managed to get disqualified from 87 games for six fouls. If he had been a starter for most of his career, he might have really left a mark on the game. As it is, however, he ranks just tenth on the all-time list. Who ranks ahead of him?

1) _____   6) _____
2) _____   7) _____
3) _____   8) _____
4) _____   9) _____
5) _____

Flash Followup

1) _____ They say George Mikan used to know how to use his elbows. But I don't know. A teammate of his was ejected from 127 games for personal reasons. Who was that Laker cornerman?

90. NOTHING PERSONAL

Paul Silas was pretty good at ranking tenth. He also placed tenth on the all-time list of the players with the most personal fouls. Who were the nine players—all but two of them retired—who got detected more times by the league's referees?

1) ——————   6) ——————
2) ——————   7) ——————
3) ——————   8) ——————
4) ——————   9) ——————
5) ——————

Flash Followup

1) —————— Who got whistled an all-time high 3,855 times?

91. MOST GAMES

Wilt Chamberlain played in 1,045 career games. But nine other courtmen—all but one of them retired—played in more games than "The Big Dipper." How many of them can you name?

1) _____   6) _____
2) _____   7) _____
3) _____   8) _____
4) _____   9) _____
5) _____

Flash Followup

1) _____ Who played in the most (1,270) games?

92. MVP AWARDS

Thirteen players have won Most Valuable Player awards since the honor was initiated in 1955–56. Spaces are provided for the number of players (for each team) who copped the coveted award. All you have to do is identify the players. There are 14 answers. One of the players won the MVP award with two different teams; one of them won it twice with the same team.

1) Boston   _____
2) Boston   _____
3) Boston   _____
4) Philadelphia   _____
5) Philadelphia   _____
6) St. Louis   _____
7) Cincinnati   _____
8) Baltimore   _____
9) New York   _____
10) Milwaukee   _____
11) Buffalo   _____
12) Portland   _____
13) Houston   _____(2)
14) Los Angeles   _____

93. ONCE IS NOT ENOUGH: II

Four of the players in the preceding quiz won the MVP Award more than once. Can you match them up with the number of times that they did it?

1) _____ (6)   3) _____ (4)
2) _____ (5)   4) _____ (2)

94. SHOOTING HIGHS

Below you will find the single-game scoring records (in regulation time) of 23 professional teams. Fill in the blanks with the respective team players who hold these records. Records of previous franchises count.

1) Warriors   _____ (100)
2) Lakers   _____ (71)
3) Suns   _____ (49)
4) Trail Blazers   _____ (51)*
5) Clippers   _____ (52)*
6) SuperSonics   _____ (58)
7) Mavericks   _____ (31)
8) Nuggets   _____ (73)
9) Rockets   _____ (57)
10) Kings   _____ (59)
11) Spurs   _____ (63)
12) Jazz   _____ (68)
13) Celtics   _____ (51)
14) Nets   _____ (63)
15) Knicks   _____ (57)
16) 76ers   _____ (68)
17) Bullets   _____ (56)
18) Hawks   _____ (57)**
19) Bucks   _____ (55)
20) Bulls   _____ (56)
21) Cavaliers   _____ (50)
22) Pistons   _____ (54)
23) Pacers   _____ (58)

* They did it twice.
** Two players share record.

123

95. THE ASSISTMEN

Below are listed 23 NBA teams and their single-game assist records. Fill in the blanks with the respective players who hold the club records. Records of previous franchises count.

1) Warriors   _____ (28)
2) Lakers   _____ (23)
3) Suns   _____ (19)
4) Trail Blazers   _____ (17)
5) Clippers   _____ (25)
6) SuperSonics   _____ (19)*
7) Mavericks   _____ (16)*
8) Nuggets   _____ (23)
9) Rockets   _____ (22)*
10) Kings   _____ (22)**
11) Spurs   _____ (16)
12) Jazz   _____ (19)
13) Celtics   _____ (28)
14) Nets   _____ (29)
15) Knicks   _____ (21)
16) 76ers   _____ (21)
17) Bullets   _____ (24)
18) Hawks   _____ (19)**
19) Bulls   _____ (21)
20) Cavaliers   _____ (20)**
21) Pistons   _____ (25)*
22) Pacers   _____ (20)
23) Bucks   _____ (22)

* They did it twice.
** Two players share record.

96. THE BOARDMEN

Below are teams and their single-game rebounding records. Fill in the blanks with the respective players who hold these marks. Records of previous franchises count.

1) Warriors ———— (55)
2) Lakers ———— (42)
3) Suns ———— (27)
4) Trail Blazers ———— (27)
5) Clippers ———— (32)
6) SuperSonics ———— (30)
7) Mavericks ———— (18)
8) Nuggets ———— (31)
9) Rockets ———— (35)
10) Kings ———— (40)
11) Spurs ———— (35)
12) Jazz ———— (27)
13) Celtics ———— (51)
14) Nets ———— (33)
15) Knicks ———— (33)
16) 76crs ———— (43)
17) Bullets ———— (37)
18) Hawks ———— (35)*
19) Bulls ———— (37)
20) Cavaliers ———— (25)
21) Pistons ———— (33)
22) Pacers ———— (37)
23) Bucks ———— (33)

* He did it twice.

97. CLUB'S ALL-TIME POINT LEADERS

How many of the all-time point leaders can you name for the clubs that are listed below? A blank within the parentheses indicates that the player in question is still active for that team. Records of previous franchises count.

1) Hawks   _____ (20,880)
2) Celtics   _____ (26,395)
3) Bulls   _____ (12,623)
4) Cavaliers   _____ (10,265)
5) Mavericks   _____ ( )
6) Nuggets   _____ ( )
7) Pistons   _____ (15,488)
8) Warriors   _____ (17,783)
9) Rockets   _____ ( )
10) Pacers   _____ (12,118)
11) Kings   _____ (22,009)
12) Lakers   _____ (25,192)
13) Bucks   _____ (14,211)
14) Nets   _____ (7,202)
15) Knicks   _____ (14,617)
16) Sixers   _____ (21,586)
17) Suns   _____ (12,060)
18) Blazers   _____ (9,732)
19) Spurs   _____ ( )
20) Clippers   _____ (12,143)
21) SuperSonics   _____ ( )
22) Jazz   _____ (7,324)
23) Bullets   _____ (15,551)

98. CLUB'S ALL-TIME ASSIST LEADERS

How many of the all-time assist leaders can you name for the clubs that are listed below? A blank within the parentheses indicates that the player in question is still active for that team. Records of previous franchises count.

1) Hawks ——————— (3,048)
2) Celtics ——————— (6,945)
3) Bulls ——————— (3,676)
4) Cavaliers ——————— (2,115)
5) Mavericks ——————— (   )
6) Nuggets ——————— (1,953)
7) Pistons ——————— (4,330)
8) Warriors ——————— (4,845)
9) Rockets ——————— (   )
10) Pacers ——————— (2,999)
11) Kings ——————— (7,721)
12) Lakers ——————— (6,238)
13) Bucks ——————— (2,156)
14) Nets ——————— (2,251)
15) Knicks ——————— (4,791)
16) 76ers ——————— (4,540)
17) Suns ——————— (2,399)
18) Blazers ——————— (1,647)
19) Spurs ——————— (2,406)
20) Clippers ——————— (3,306)
21) Sonics ——————— (2,777)
22) Jazz ——————— (1,844)
23) Bullets ——————— (3,822)

99. CLUB'S ALL-TIME REBOUND LEADERS

How many of the all-time rebound leaders can you name for the clubs that are listed below? A blank within the parentheses indicates that the player in question is still active for that team. Records of previous franchises count.

1) Hawks ———— (12,851)
2) Celtics ———— (21,620)
3) Bulls ———— (5,745)
4) Cavaliers ———— (3,790)
5) Mavericks ———— (   )
6) Nuggets ———— (5,261)
7) Pistons ———— (8,033)
8) Warriors ———— (12,771)
9) Rockets ———— (   )
10) Pacers ———— (9,045)
11) Kings ———— (8,831)
12) Lakers ———— (11,463)
13) Bucks ———— (7,167)
14) Nets ———— (2,990)
15) Knicks ———— (8,414)
16) 76ers ———— (11,256)
17) Suns ———— (3,637)
18) Blazers ———— (4,086)
19) Spurs ———— (4,106)
20) Clippers ———— (4,229)
21) Sonics ———— (3,954)
22) Jazz ———— (1,865)
23) Bullets ———— (13,769)

100. NBA GAME RECORDS

Fill in the blanks.

1) _____ Who twice made 18 consecutive field goals?
2) _____ Who made 28 free throws in a regular-season game?
3) _____ Who made 19 consecutive free throws in one game?
4) _____ Who scored 15 consecutive points?
5) _____ Who dished out 29 assists?
6) _____ Who committed 8 personal fouls in one game?

101. NBA SEASON RECORDS

1) _____ Who scored 4,029 points in one season?
2) _____ Who averaged 50.4 points per game?
3) _____ Who sank 90 three-point field goals?
4) _____ Who had a field goal percentage of .727?
5) _____ Who had a three-point field goal percentage of .443?
6) _____ Who made 840 free throws?
7) _____ Who shot .958 from the foul line?
8) _____ Who had 2,149 rebounds?
9) _____ Who converted 1,099 assists?
10) _____ Who committed 367 personal fouls?

102. PLAYOFF GAME RECORDS: PRELIMINARY SERIES

1) _____ Who scored 56 points in one game?
2) _____ Who sank 30 free throws?
3) _____ Who sank 18 free throws in a row?
4) _____ Who pulled down 41 rebounds?
5) _____ Who is the retired center who recorded 19 assists?
6) _____ Who is the retired guard who served up 19 assists?
7) _____ Who is the present-day player who recorded 19 assists?

103. PLAYOFF GAME RECORDS: CHAMPIONSHIP SERIES

Fill in the blanks.

1) _____ Who scored 61 points?
2) _____ Who took 48 shots?
3) _____ Who sank 19 free throws?
4) _____ Who twice pulled down 40 rebounds?
5) _____ Who twice handed off 19 assists?
6) _____ Who else had a 19-assist game?

104. ABA SINGLE-GAME RECORDS

Match the players with the single-game marks that they hold.

1) __ Larry Miller
2) __ Les Selvage
3) __ Tony Jackson
4) __ Artis Gilmore
5) __ Larry Brown
6) __ Rick Barry

a) Most rebounds (40)
b) Most consecutive free throws (23)
c) Most points (67)
d) Most assists (23)
e) Most three-point field goals (10)
f) Most free throws made (24)

105. ABA SEASON RECORDS

Match the players with the season records that they hold.

1) __ Dan Issel
2) __ Charlie Scott
3) __ Bobby Jones
4) __ Louie Dampier
5) __ Billy Shepherd
6) __ Mack Calvin
7) __ Spencer Haywood
8) __ Don Buse
9) __ Gene Moore

a) Most three-point field goals made (199)
b) Most points (2,538)
c) Most disqualifications (25)
d) Highest scoring average (34.58)
e) Most assists (689)
f) Highest free throw percentage (.896)
g) Highest field goal percentage (.605)
h) Highest three-point field goal percentage (.420)
i) Most rebounds (1,637)

106. ABA CAREER RECORDS

Fill in the blanks from the following names: Louie Dampier, Mel Daniels, Julius Erving, Jim Logan, and Mack Calvin.

1) _____ Who scored the most (13,726) points?

2) _____ Who had the highest average (28.7) for at least 250 games?

3) _____ Who made the most two-point field goals?

4) _____ Who made the most (794) three-point field goals?

5) _____ Who made the most (3,554) free throws?

6) _____ Who pulled down the most (9,494) rebounds?

7) _____ Who handed off the most (4,084) assists?

8) _____ Who played the most (27,770) minutes?

9) _____ Who committed the most (1,689) personal fouls?

10) _____ Who earned the most (43) disqualifications?

11) _____ Who played the most (728) games?

107. MULTIPLE ABA FIRST-TEAM SELECTIONS

All of the players who are listed below were named to the ABA (first-team) All-Star squad at least once. Nine of them were named to the team on multiple occasions. Mark a check next to the name of each multiple selectee.

1) Connie Hawkins
2) Doug Moe
3) Mel Daniels
4) Larry Jones
5) Rick Barry
6) James Jones
7) Spencer Haywood
8) Mack Calvin
9) Charlie Scott
10) Dan Issel
11) Artis Gilmore
12) Don Freeman
13) Bill Melchionni
14) Billy Cunningham
15) Julius Erving
16) Warren Jabali
17) George McGinnis
18) Ron Boone
19) Billy Knight
20) James Silas

108. ABA'S WHO'S WHO

1) _____ Who was named to the ABA First-Team All-Star squad a record five times?

2) _____ Who are the three players who were named to the squad four times?

3) _____

4) _____

5) _____ Who was the first MVP (1968) of the ABA?

6) _____ Who was the first Rookie of the Year?

7) _____ Who won the MVP and Rookie of the Year awards in different (1969 and 1968) years?

8) _____ Who are the two players to win the MVP and Rookie of the Year awards in the same year?

9) _____

10) _____ Who won the MVP Award a record three times in a row?

11) _____ Who is the only other player to win the MVP Award more than once?

109. A MATTER OF ASSOCIATION

Twenty-two of the players listed below began their careers in the NBA and finished them in the ABA, 16 of them started their careers in the ABA and concluded (or will conclude) them in the NBA, and 11 of them began their careers in the NBA, switched to the ABA, and terminated them back in the NBA. Next to each name write NBA for the first group of players, ABA for the second group, and NAN for the third group.

1) John Barnhill   _____
2) Joe Caldwell   _____
3) Allan Bristow   _____
3) Ron Boone   _____
5) Terry Driscoll   _____
6) Mack Calvin   _____
7) Jim Chones   _____
8) Steve Mix   _____
9) Coby Dietrick   _____
10) Cliff Hagan   _____
11) Art Heyman   _____
12) Wayne Hightower   _____
13) Mike Gale   _____
14) Don Adams   _____
15) Bobby Jones   _____
16) Billy Knight   _____
17) Roger Brown   _____
18) Tom Hoover   _____
19) Neil Johnson   _____
20) Ed Manning   _____
21) Maurice Lucas   _____
22) Don Chaney   _____
23) Moses Malone   _____
24) Swen Nater   _____
25) Tom Owens   _____
26) Billy Cunningham   _____
27) Billy McGill   _____
28) Billy Paultz   _____
29) Bill Melchionni   _____
30) Jack Moreland   _____
31) Nick Jones   _____
32) Erwin Mueller   _____
33) Dave Robisch   _____
34) Flynn Robinson   _____
35) Adrian Smith   _____
36) Wali Jones   _____
37) Tom Thacker   _____

38) Al Tucker   _____
39) Brian Taylor   _____
40) Chuck Terry   _____
41) Chico Vaughn   _____
42) Dave Twardzik   _____
43) Ben Warley   _____
44) Art Williams   _____
45) John Williamson   _____
46) Bernie Williams   _____
47) Zelmo Beaty   _____
48) Tom Workman   _____
49) Tom Hoover   _____

110. TWO-DIMENSIONAL PLAYERS

Match the following NBA players with the teams with which they once played in the ABA: Dick Barnett, Connie Hawkins, Rick Barry, Mel Daniels, Spencer Haywood, Dan Issel, Artis Gilmore, Billy Cunningham, Julius Erving, and Wilt Chamberlain.

1) _____ Minnesota Muskies
2) _____ Cleveland Pipers
3) _____ San Diego Conquistadors
4) _____ Virginia Squires
5) _____ Pittsburgh Rens
6) _____ Carolina Cougars
7) _____ Kentucky Colonels
8) _____ Denver Rockets
9) _____ Oakland Oaks
10) _____ Kentucky Colonels

111. SUPER (ABA) SCORERS

Six of the players in the history of the ABA averaged 30-or-more points a game in one season. How many of them can you name?

1) ——————   4) ——————
2) ——————   5) ——————
3) ——————   6) ——————

Flash Followup

1) —————— Who was the one player to do it twice?

112. FIRST-TEAM ALL STARS

Which member of the following pairs of players (has) made the First-Team All-Star squad more times than the other? Mark a check before his name.

_____ Joe Fulks	_____ Bob Feerick
_____ Max Zaslofsky	_____ Ed Macauley
_____ Ed Sadowski	_____ Jim Pollard
_____ Alex Groza	_____ Bones McKinney
_____ Stan Miasek	_____ Spencer Haywood
_____ Bob Davies	_____ Paul Arizin
_____ Ralph Beard	_____ Dave Bing
_____ Bill Sharman	_____ Bill Russell
_____ George Mikan	_____ Rick Barry
_____ Oscar Robertson	_____ Bob Cousy
_____ Elgin Baylor	_____ Kareem Abdul-Jabbar
_____ George Yardley	_____ Pete Maravich
_____ Neil Johnston	_____ Elvin Hayes
_____ Bob Pettit	_____ Dolph Schayes
_____ Jerry West	_____ Wilt Chamberlain
_____ Jerry Lucas	_____ Walt Frazier
_____ Billy Cunningham	_____ John Havlicek

Flash Followup

Four of the above players were named to the First-Team All-Star club a record-tying ten times. Which ones?

1) _____   3) _____
2) _____   4) _____

113. ONCE A BRIDESMAID...

One half of the following players made the First-Team All-Star club *once*; the other half never made the First Team but earned Second-Team honors at least three times: John Logan, Vern Mikkelsen, Howie Dallmar, Bobby Wanzer, Harry Gallatin, Slater Martin, Larry Foust, Gene Shue, Wes Unseld, Maurice Stokes, Earl Monroe, Connie Hawkins, Richie Guerin, Willis Reed, Tommy Heinsohn, Hal Greer, Gail Goodrich, Sam Jones, Dave Cowens, Bob McAdoo, George McGinnis, and Gus Johnson. Place the first-team members in the left-hand column below and the second-team members in the right-hand column.

First Team		*Second Team*	
1) _____	7) _____	1) _____	7) _____
2) _____	8) _____	2) _____	8) _____
3) _____	9) _____	3) _____	9) _____
4) _____	10) _____	4) _____	10) _____
5) _____	11) _____	5) _____	11) _____
6) _____		6) _____	

Flash Followup

1) _____ Who was the player who made the second team *seven* times but never made the first team?

2) _____ Who were the other four players who made the second team *more* than three times?

3) _____

4) _____

5) _____

114. ALL-STAR MVPS

From the multiple choice groups below select the NBA All-Star Game MVP of the respective year.

1) ___ 1951 a) Ed Macauley b) Joe Fulks c) George Mikan

2) ___ 1952 a) Max Zaslofsky b) Paul Arizin c) Jim Pollard

3) ___ 1953 a) Neil Johnston b) George Mikan c) Bob Cousy

4) ___ 1954 a) Bob Cousy b) Bill Sharman c) Arnie Risen

5) ___ 1955 a) Bob Pettit b) George Yardley c) Bill Sharman

6) ___ 1956 a) Bob Pettit b) Maurice Stokes c) Dolph Schayes

7) ___ 1957 a) Bob Cousy b) Tom Heinsohn c) Jack Twyman

8) ___ 1958 a) Elgin Baylor b) Slater Martin c) Bob Pettit

* 9) ___ 1959 a) Elgin Baylor b) Bill Russell c) Bob Pettit

10) ___ 1960 a) Tom Gola b) Wilt Chamberlain c) Cliff Hagan

11) ___ 1961 a) Oscar Robertson b) Elgin Baylor c) Clyde Lovellette

12) ___ 1962 a) Bailey Howell b) Paul Arizin c) Bob Pettit

13) ___ 1963 a) Bill Russell b) Jerry West c) Wilt Chamberlain

14) ___ 1964 a) Elgin Baylor b) Jerry West c) Oscar Robertson

15) __ 1965) a) Jerry Lucas b) Nate Thurmond c) Willis Reed

16) __ 1966 a) Chet Walker b) Rudy LaRusso c) Adrian Smith

17) __ 1967 a) John Havlicek b) Rick Barry c) Guy Rodgers

18) __ 1968 a) Hal Greer b) Bob Boozer c) Dave DeBusschere

19) __ 1969 a) Gus Johnson b) Oscar Robertson c) Lou Hudson

20) __ 1970 a) Willis Reed b) Billy Cunningham c) Lenny Wilkens

21) __ 1971 a) Walt Frazier b) Lenny Wilkens c) Earl Monroe

22) __ 1972 a) Bob Lanier b) Bob Love c) Jerry West

23) __ 1973 a) Elvin Hayes b) Dave Cowens c) Dave Bing

24) __ 1974 a) Pete Maravich b) Gail Goodrich c) Bob Lanier

25) __ 1975 a) Jo Jo White b) Spencer Haywood c) Walt Frazier

26) __ 1976 a) Dave Bing b) John Havlicek c) Bob McAdoo

27) __ 1977 a) Julius Erving b) David Thompson c) Dan Issel

28) __ 1978 a) Bill Walton b) George Gervin c) Randy Smith

29) __ 1979 a) Kareem Abdul-Jabbar b) David Thompson c) Calvin Murphy

30) __ 1980 a) Dennis Johnson b) George Gervin c) Moses Malone

31) __ 1981 a) Larry Bird b) Nate Archibald c) Julius Erving

32) __ 1982 a) Larry Bird b) Magic Johnson c) Gus Williams

* Two players tied for the award. Name both players to score.

115. DOUBLE-DIGIT ASSISTMEN

Only four players have handed off ten or more assists in one game in an All-Star contest. How many of them can you name? All of them are retired.

1) _____   3) _____
2) _____   4) _____

Flash Followup

1) _____ Who recorded a record 14 assists in one game?
2) _____ Who were the two players to record ten or more assists in an ABA All Star Game?

116. THE BOUNDERS

Four players have hauled down 20 or more rebounds in an NBA All-Star Game. How many of them can you name? All of them are retired.

1) _____   3) _____
2) _____   4) _____

Flash Followup

1) _____ Who recorded a league-high 27 rebounds?
2) _____ Who was the only player to record 20 or more rebounds in an ABA All-Star Game?

117. 30-POINT SHOOTERS

Seven players—three of whom are still active—have scored 30 or more points in an NBA All-Star Game. How many of them can you name?

1) _____   5) _____
2) _____   6) _____
3) _____   7) _____
4) _____

Flash Followup

1) _____ Who scored a record 42 points in one game?
2) _____ Who was the only player to score 30 points in an ABA All-Star Game?

118. ALL-STAR MATCHUPS

Use the following names to fill in the blanks below: Oscar Robertson, Bob Pettit, Rick Barry, John Havlicek, Wilt Chamberlain, Elgin Baylor, Archie Clark, Bob Cousy, David Thompson, Dolph Schayes, and Jerry West. The names may be used more than once.

1) _____ Wilt Chamberlain, Bob Cousy, and who else performed in a record 13 games?
2) _____ Who played a record 388 minutes?
3) _____ Who took a record 193 shots, 21 more than his closest runner-up?
4) _____ Who made a record 88 shots?

143

5) _____ Who, in addition to Elgin Baylor, attempted a record 98 free throws?

6) _____ Who made a record 78 free throws?

7) _____ Who, shooting a minimum of ten free throws, hit a record 1.000 from the line?

8) _____ Who committed a record 41 personal fouls?

9) _____ Who pulled down a record 197 rebounds?

10) _____ Who pulled down a record 178 rebounds by a forward?

11) _____ Who handed off a record 86 assists?

12) _____ Who was the forward who was named to the First Team six times and the Second Team six times?

13) _____ Who committed a record five personal fouls in one half?

14) _____ Who, among the following four, played a record-tying 42 minutes in one game: Jerry West, Bob Cousy, Paul Arizin, or Elgin Baylor?

15) _____ Who attempted a record 27 field goals in one game?

A NINE-POINT OVERTIME IS JUST ANOTHER DAY'S WORK

Sometimes there just doesn't seem to be any justice. Occasionally a player—even a great player like John Havlicek—will turn in just about the greatest game of his career and simply go down in the record books as just a footnote to history.

Havlicek's performance in the sixth game of the 1973–74 playoff confrontation between the Celtics and the Bucks is an example of the injustice we're talking about. "Hondo" was almost invincible. *Almost!*

The Boston swingman showed a huge television audience that hustle pays off. With 13 seconds remaining in the first overtime period, he missed a 15-footer; but he followed up the miss, rebounded his own shot, and tied the score at 90 just before the buzzer.

As events turned out, however, he was just warming up for the second overtime period. He scored nine of the Celtics' 11 points. (Nine points in one overtime period, as you know by now, is a playoff record.) With seven seconds left, he scored his last two points on a baseline jumper that just cleared Kareem Abdul-Jabbar's sky-bound fingers. The Celtics led 102–101.

Boston had to win, millions of television viewers told themselves. Destiny, they reasoned, could not deny Havlicek his moment of glory. So much for destiny!

Milwaukee hurriedly got the ball up court; and a five-year player, with the poise of an "old pro," dribbled into the deep right corner and lofted a soft hook shot that ripped the cords with the game-winning basket. The Bucks won 103–102.

The percentages, before that shot, seemed tilted in Havlicek's favor. But a seemingly bad-percentage shot switched the odds in Milwaukee's favor.

Who took that "bad" percentage shot?

Answer: Kareem Abdul-Jabbar

THIRD-PERIOD SCORE

(Total just the third-period points.)

Points

You __ The NBA __

Games

You __ The NBA __

THE FOURTH QUARTER

119. CAREER POINTS

There are 64 players listed below. Nineteen of them scored less than 10,000 career points, 20 of them scored between 10,- and 15,000 points, 17 of them scored between 15,- and 20,000 points, and 8 of them scored more than 20,000 points. Can you determine in which placements the players belong?

Paul Arizin
Dick Barnett
Rick Barry
Elgin Baylor
Zelmo Beaty
Walt Bellamy
Bill Bradley
Fred Carter
Larry Costello
Bob Cousy
Dave Cowens
Billy Cunningham
Bob Davies
Dave DeBusschere
Connie Dierking
Terry Dischinger
Wayne Embry

Neil Johnston
Sam Jones
John Kerr
Butch Komives
Kevin Loughery
Bob Love
Clyde Lovellette
Ed Macauley
Pete Maravich
Jack Marin
Slater Martin
Jon McGlocklin
Dick McGuire
Jim McMillian
George Mikan
Earl Monroe
Don Nelson

Ray Felix
Walt Frazier
Joe Fulks
Harry Gallatin
Tom Gola
Gail Goodrich
Hal Greer
Rich Guerin
Cliff Hagan
Happy Hairston
John Havlicek
Spencer Haywood
Tom Heinsohn
Bailey Howell
Lou Hudson

Bob Pettit
Andy Phillip
Jim Pollard
Frank Ramsey
Willis Reed
Oscar Robertson
Bill Russell
Dolph Schayes
Bill Sharman
Nate Thurmond
Jack Twyman
Chet Walker
Jerry West
Lenny Wilkens
George Yardley

Below 10,000

1) _____   11) _____
2) _____   12) _____
3) _____   13) _____
4) _____   14) _____
5) _____   15) _____
6) _____   16) _____
7) _____   17) _____
8) _____   18) _____
9) _____   19) _____
10) _____

Between 10,000 and 15,000

1) _____   11) _____
2) _____   12) _____
3) _____   13) _____
4) _____   14) _____
5) _____   15) _____
6) _____   16) _____
7) _____   17) _____
8) _____   18) _____
9) _____   19) _____
10) _____   20) _____

Between 15,000 and 20,000

1) _____	10) _____
2) _____	11) _____
3) _____	12) _____
4) _____	13) _____
5) _____	14) _____
6) _____	15) _____
7) _____	16) _____
8) _____	17) _____
9) _____	

Above 20,000

1) _____	5) _____
2) _____	6) _____
3) _____	7) _____
4) _____	8) _____

120. CAREER AVERAGES

Nine of the players listed on Quiz 119 "Career Points" posted career averages of 8 to 12 points a game, 17 of them registered marks of 12 to 16 points a game, 25 of them chalked up numbers of 16 to 20 points a game, seven of them logged stats of 20 to 24 points a game, and six of them ripped the cords for 24 or more points a game. Can you place the players according to the hierarchy of career points found below?

Eight to 12 Points

1) _____	5) _____
2) _____	6) _____
3) _____	7) _____
4) _____	8) _____
	9) _____

12 to 16 Points

1) ———	10) ———
2) ———	11) ———
3) ———	12) ———
4) ———	13) ———
5) ———	14) ———
6) ———	15) ———
7) ———	16) ———
8) ———	17) ———
9) ———	

16 to 20 Points

1) ———	14) ———
2) ———	15) ———
3) ———	16) ———
4) ———	17) ———
5) ———	18) ———
6) ———	19) ———
7) ———	20) ———
8) ———	21) ———
9) ———	22) ———
10) ———	23) ———
11) ———	24) ———
12) ———	25) ———
13) ———	

20 to 24 Points

1) ———	5) ———
2) ———	6) ———
3) ———	7) ———
4) ———	

24 or More Points

1) ———	4) ———
2) ———	5) ———
3) ———	6) ———

121. 30-POINT SEASONS

Name the nine of the following 16 players who averaged 30 or more points *only* once: Kareem Adul-Jabbar, Nate Archibald, Julius Erving, Dan Issel, Bob McAdoo, Rick Barry, Elgin Baylor, Walt Bellamy, Wilt Chamberlain, Connie Hawkins, Spencer Haywood, Pete Maravich, Bob Pettit, Oscar Robertson, Jack Twyman, and Jerry West.

1) _____   6) _____
2) _____   7) _____
3) _____   8) _____
4) _____   9) _____
5) _____

122. MULTIPLE 30-POINT SEASONS

Seven of the players in the preceding quiz, "30-Point Seasons," averaged 30 or more points a season on more than one occasion. Match them with the number of times that they did it. In case of ties, the order does not count.

1) _____ (7)   5) _____ (4)
2) _____ (6)   6) _____ (3)
3) _____ (4)   7) _____ (3)
4) _____ (4)

123. GOOD IS JUST NOT GOOD ENOUGH

All of the players who are listed below (are) were good foul shooters. Ten of them sank more than 650 charity-stripe tries in one season. Mark a check next to the names of those who did.

1) Rick Barry
2) Elgin Baylor
3) Dave Bing
4) Larry Cannon
5) Wilt Chamberlain
6) Don Freeman
7) Richie Guerin
8) Nate Archibald
9) Mack Calvin
10) Adrian Dantley
11) Lloyd Free
12) Dan Issel
13) Bob McAdoo
14) Connie Hawkins
15) Bailey Howell
16) Bob Pettit
17) Oscar Robertson
18) Dolph Schayes
19) Jerry West

Flash Followup

Five players in the history of the NBA have sunk more than 6,000 free throws. How many of them can you name?

1) _____   4) _____
2) _____   5) _____
3) _____

124. THE RIGHT HEIGHT

The fifty retired players who are listed below ranged in height from 5-8 to 7-2. They had varied abilities, also. But each of them stood tall in the pro ranks. Can you match them with their proper mountain ranges?

Ralph Beard
Henry Finkel
Wilt Chamberlain
Bill Walton
Paul Arizin
Guy Rodgers
Marvin Barnes
Fred Scolari
Lucius Allen
Chet Walker
Mel Counts
Ron Taylor
Alex Groza
Don Chaney
Joe Hamilton
Kenny Sailors
Walter Dukes
Rick Barry
Larry Siegfried
John Kerr
Ernie Calverley
Dave Newmark
Al Cervi
Andy Phillip
Len Chappell

Mel Riebe
Johnny Egan
Frank Brian
Chick Reiser
Luke Witte
Connie Dierking
Mel Daniels
Greg Fillmore
Al Bianchi
Sonny Hertzberg
Leroy Ellis
Larry Foust
Elgin Baylor
Vince Boryla
Fred Carter
Slater Martin
Sihugo Green
Archie Clark
Ed Conlin
Swede Halbrook
Nate Thurmond
Dolph Schayes
Bob Davies
Howie Dallmar
Jim McDaniels

7-0 to 7-3

1) _____
2) _____
3) _____
4) _____
5) _____
6) _____
7) _____
8) _____
9) _____
10) _____

6-4 to 6-7

1) _____
2) _____
3) _____
4) _____
5) _____
6) _____
7) _____
8) _____
9) _____
10) _____

6-8 to 6-11

1) _____
2) _____
3) _____
4) _____
5) _____
6) _____
7) _____
8) _____
9) _____
10) _____

6-0 to 6-3

1) _____
2) _____
3) _____
4) _____
5) _____
6) _____
7) _____
8) _____
9) _____
10) _____

5-8 to 5-11

1) _____
2) _____
3) _____
4) _____
5) _____
6) _____
7) _____
8) _____
9) _____
10) _____

125. MATCHING NICKNAMES

Match the following (retired) players with their nicknames that are listed below:

Kevin Connors	Robert Boozer
Earl Lloyd	Ephraim Rocha
Rodney Hundley	Dave Stallworth
Harold Hairston	Harry Gallatin
Howard Komives	Howard Schultz
Don Watts	Harry Boykoff
Jeff Mullins	Nat Clifton
Joe Fulks	Bob Davies
Andrew Levane	Billy Cunningham
Oscar Robertson	Wilt Chamberlain
Joseph White	Jerry West
Joseph Reiser	Paul Arizin
Kevin Loughery	Adrian Smith
Paul Hoffman	Robert Zawoluk
Joe Graboski	Max Zaslofsky
Harry Grant	Bobby Smith
Bill McGill	Joe Caldwell
Arthur Spector	Harley Swift
Jim Barnes	Don Carlson
Al Cervi	William van Breda Kolff
George Glamack	Don Chaney
William Holzman	Tom Washington
Bob Warren	Sidney Hertzberg
John Havlicek	Art Williams
Zelmo Beaty	Leslie Hunter
Tom Sanders	Earl Monroe
Wayne Embry	Wallace Jones
Jerry Sloan	Arnold Risen
Ken Sears	James King

Walt Frazier   Richard McGuire
Walt Bellamy   James Loscutoff
Frank Saul   Don Meineke
Horace McKinney   Robert Kinney
Robert Leonard   Charles Nash
Ed Macauley   Leo Klier
Slater Martin   David Lattin

1) "Bad News" _____   30) "Butch" _____
2) "Big Z" _____   31) "Big Daddy" _____
3) "Bells" _____   32) "Slick" _____
4) "Bullet Bob" _____   33) "Fuzzy" _____
5) "Big Hesh" _____   34) "Big Cat" _____
6) "Pogo" _____   35) "Jungle Jim" _____
7) "Swede" _____   36) "Murph" _____
8) "Digger" _____   37) "Easy Ed" _____
9) "Duck" _____   38) "Dugie" _____
10) "Sweetwater" _____   39) "The Hill" _____
11) "Chuck" _____   40) "Tricky Dick" _____
12) "Goose" _____
13) "Clyde" _____   _____
14) "Jumpin' Joe"   41) "Bones" _____
                           42) "Monk" _____
_____   43) "The Pearl" _____
15) "The Horse" _____   44) "Pork Chop" _____
16) "Blind Bomber"   45) "Cotton" _____
                           46) "Chick" _____
_____   47) "Stilts" _____
17) "Grabbo" _____   48) "The Big O" _____
18) "Bud" _____   49) "Red" _____
19) "Happy" _____   50) "Satch" _____
20) "Hondo" _____   51) "Pep" _____
21) "Sonny" _____   52) "Stretch" _____
22) "Bear" _____   53) "Big Cat" _____
23) "Red" _____   54) "Spider" _____
24) "Hot Rod" _____   55) "Odie" _____
25) "Big Game" _____   56) "Bingo" _____
26) "Wah Wah" _____   57) "Speed" _____
27) "Country" _____   58) "The Rave" _____
28) "High Pocket"   59) "Skeeter" _____
                           60) "Butch" _____
_____
29) "Crystal" _____

61) "Colonel" _____   68) "Pitchin' Paul"
62) "Trooper" _____   _____
63) "Slick" _____   69) "Mr. Clutch" _____
64) "Jo Jo" _____   70) "The Stilt" _____
65) "Hambone" _____   71) "The Kangaroo Kid"
66) "Slats" _____   72) "The Harrisburg
67) "Zeke" _____   Houdini" _____

126. OLD NBA NUMBERS

Match the following retired players with the numbers (in parentheses below) that they made recognizable in NBA play: Billy Cunningham, Bob Pettit, Dolph Schayes, Wes Unseld, Oscar Robertson (Bucks), Ed Macauley (Hawks), Pete Maravich, Jerry West, Wilt Chamberlain, Bill Sharman, Neil Johnston, Bill Russell, Walt Frazier, K.C. Jones, John Havlicek, Phil Chenier, Slater Martin, Lenny Wilkens, Joe Fulks, Jack Twyman, Wayne Embry, Cazzie Russell, Paul Silas, Clyde Lovellette, Chet Walker, George Mikan, Bob Davies, Spencer Haywood, Paul Arizin, Dave Cowens, Rick Barry, Frank Ramsey, George Yardley, Bob Cousy, Willis Reed, Cliff Hagan, Sweetwater Clifton, Elgin Baylor, Dick Barnett, Earl Monroe, Tom Gola, Jerry Lucas, Dave DeBusschere, and Red Holzman. Some of them wore the same number.

1) _____ (1)   9) _____ (11)
2) _____ (4)   10) _____ (11)
3) _____ (6)   11) _____ (12)
4) _____ (6)   12) _____ (12)
5) _____ (7)   13) _____ (13)
6) _____ (9)   14) _____ (14)
7) _____ (10)   15) _____ (15)
8) _____ (10)   16) _____ (15)

17) _____ (16)		31) _____ (24)
18) _____ (16)		32) _____ (24)
19) _____ (16)		33) _____ (25)
20) _____ (17)		34) _____ (25)
21) _____ (18)		35) _____ (27)
22) _____ (19)		36) _____ (28)
23) _____ (19)		37) _____ (32)
24) _____ (19)		38) _____ (33)
25) _____ (20)		39) _____ (34)
26) _____ (21)		40) _____ (35)
27) _____ (22)		41) _____ (41)
28) _____ (22)		42) _____ (44)
29) _____ (22)		43) _____ (45)
30) _____ (23)		44) _____ (99)

127. PLAYER POSITIONS

Below are listed forty retired players. All you have to
do is to write their positions—"Guard," "Forward," or
"Center"—next to their names. If you're the "pro" that
we think you are, you're about to go to the fast break.
Some of them were swingmen. But they're more recognizable at one position than they are at another.

1) Dick Barnett   _____
2) Rick Barry   _____
3) Walt Bellamy   _____
4) Ralph Beard   _____
5) Larry Brown   _____
6) Dave Cowens   _____
7) Dave DeBusschere   _____
8) Harry Gallatin   _____
9) Gail Goodrich   _____
10) Spencer Haywood   _____

11) Darrall Imhoff   _____
12) Neil Johnston   _____
13) Sam Jones   _____
14) Clyde Lovellette   _____
15) Jerry Lucas   _____
16) Ray Lumpp   _____
17) Jack Marin   _____
18) Jack McMahon   _____
19) George Mikan   _____
20) Don Nelson   _____
21) Don Otten   _____
22) Jim Pollard   _____
23) Willis Reed   _____
24) Guy Rodgers   _____
25) Bob Feerick   _____
26) Ed Sadowski   _____
27) Dolph Schayes   _____
28) Wes Unseld   _____
29) Tom Heinsohn   _____
30) Dave Bing   _____
31) Ernie Calverley   _____
32) Max Zaslofsky   _____
33) Joe Fulks   _____
34) Bobby Wanzer   _____
35) Gus Johnson   _____
36) Connie Hawkins   _____
37) Jack Twyman   _____
38) Kenny Sailors   _____
39) Charlie Share   _____
40) Bill Walton   _____

128. COLLEGE BALL

Match the current-day players in the left-hand column with the colleges at which they played in the right-hand column.

1) __ John Lucas
2) __ Jo Jo White
3) __ Jim Chones
4) __ Spencer Haywood
5) __ Alvan Adams
6) __ Dave Twardzik
7) __ Lloyd Free
8) __ Marvin Barnes
9) __ Paul Westphal
10) __ Jim Spanarkel
11) __ David Thompson
12) __ Calvin Murphy
13) __ Phil Ford
14) __ George Gervin
15) __ Bernard King
16) __ Chris Ford
17) __ Jan van Breda Kolff
18) __ Michael Richardson
19) __ Doug Collins
20) __ Bob Dandridge
21) __ Tree Rollins
22) __ Dennis Awtrey
23) __ Campy Russell
24) __ Kent Benson
25) __ Bob Lanier

a) Marquette
b) Duke
c) Guilford
d) Eastern Michigan
e) Clemson
f) Niagara
g) St. Bonaventure
h) Norfolk State
i) Maryland
j) Michigan
k) Montana
l) USC
m) Villanova
n) Detroit
o) Illinois State
p) Providence
q) Tennessee
r) Kansas
s) North Carolina
t) Santa Clara
u) Old Dominion
v) Indiana
w) Vanderbilt
x) Oklahoma
y) North Carolina State

129. ONE-TEAM PLAYERS

Mark a check next to twenty of the players listed below who spent their entire professional careers with one team. (Their careers, by the way, lasted at least ten years each.)

Lucius Allen
Paul Arizin
Al Attles
Elgin Baylor
Al Bianchi
Tom Boerwinkle
Bob Boozer
Fred Boyd
Bill Bradley
Fred Brown
Emmette Bryant
Joe Caldwell
Ed Conlin
Larry Costello
Bob Cousy
Dave Cowens
Bob Davies
Dave DeBusschere
Connie Dierking
Bob Ferry
Larry Foust

Hal Greer
John Havlicek
Gus Johnson
Sam Jones
Curtis Perry
George Ratkovicz
Willis Reed
Bill Russell
Cazzie Russell
Satch Sanders
Woody Sauldsberry
Dolph Schayes
Charlie Scott
Paul Seymour
Jack Twyman
Bobby Wanzer
Jerry West
Jo Jo White
Lenny Wilkens
George Yardley

130. DOUBLE-DIGIT YEARS

Mark a check next to the names of 25 of the players listed below who have had careers that spanned ten or more years.

1) Paul Arizin
2) Al Attles
3) Bill Bradley
4) Emmette Bryant
5) Fred Carter
6) Al Cervi
7) Sweetwater Clifton
8) Jack Coleman
9) Dave Cowens
10) Bob Davies
11) Terry Dischinger
12) Wayne Embry
13) Ray Felix
14) Bob Ferry
15) Joe Fulks
16) Harry Gallatin
17) Jack George
18) Tom Gola
19) Happy Hairston
20) Alex Hannum
21) Connie Hawkins
22) Tom Heinsohn
23) Red Holzman
24) Buddy Jeannette
25) Neil Johnston

26) K.C. Jones
27) Wali Jones
28) Butch Komives
29) Rudy LaRusso
30) Earl Lloyd
31) Ed Macauley
32) Dick McGuire
33) Jack McMahon
34) George Mikan
35) Jack Nichols
36) Don Ohl
37) Andy Phillip
38) Jim Pollard
39) Frank Ramsey
40) Willis Reed
41) Mike Riordan
42) Fred Scolari
43) Frank Selvy
44) George Senesky
45) Gene Shue
46) Jerry Sloan
47) Dave Stallworth
48) Bobby Wanzer
49) Norm Van Lier
50) Bingo Smith

131. NEW YORK AREA SCHOOLS

New York area basketball has made a great impact on our national game. Forty professional basketball players, active and retired, are listed below. All you have to do is identify the New York area college for which they played. New York City schools that can be used are St. John's, Columbia, L.I.U., and N.Y.U. Two New Jersey schools, Seton Hall and Princeton, can also be used.

1) Harry Boykoff   _____
2) Walt Budko   _____
3) Tom Byrnes   _____
4) Gerry Calabrese   _____
5) Chuck Connors   _____
6) Bob Davies   _____
7) Mel Davis   _____
8) Leroy Ellis   _____
9) Ray Felix   _____
10) Jerry Fleishman   _____
11) Happy Hairston   _____
12) Fuzzy Levane   _____
13) Kevin Loughery   _____
14) Ray Lumpp   _____
15) Walter Dukes   _____
16) Richie Regan   _____
17) Al McGuire   _____
18) Dick McGuire   _____
19) Stan McKenzie   _____
20) Jack McMahon   _____
21) Jim McMillian   _____
22) Bill Bradley   _____
23) Bud Palmer   _____

24) Chick Reiser   ————
25) Irv Rothenberg   ————
26) Ed Sadowski   ————
27) Satch Sanders   ————
28) Pep Saul   ————
29) Billy Schaeffer   ————
30) Dolph Schayes   ————
31) Sid Tanenbaum   ————
32) Irv Torgoff   ————
33) Butch van Breda Kolff ————
34) Bobby Wanzer   ————
35) Max Zaslofsky   ————
36) Billy Paultz   ————
37) Brian Taylor   ————
38) Geoff Petrie   ————
39) Jack Garfinkel   ————
40) Whitey Macknowski ————

132. THE OLYMPIANS OF THEIR TIMES

Of the following 30 players, 17 of them played on NCAA champion teams, and 15 of them played on Olympic champs: Tom Abernethy, Jim Brewer, Michael Brooks, Kent Benson, Henry Bibby, Quinn Buckner, Tom Burleson, Ralph Drollinger, Adrian Dantley, Phil Ford, Bill Hanzlik, Darrell Griffith, Magic Johnson, Marques Johnson, Tom Henderson, Phil Hubbard, Greg Kelser, Kyle Macy, Dwight Jones, Bobby Jones, Scott May, Mitch Kupchak, Andre McCarter, Tom Lagarde, Tom McMillen, Swen Nater, Rick Robey, David Thompson, Richard Lee Washington, and Jo Jo White.

Place the NCAA champs in one column and the Olympic champs in the other column. Two of the players performed on both teams.

NCAA Champs	Olympic Champs
1) _____	1) _____
2) _____	2) _____
3) _____	3) _____
4) _____	4) _____
5) _____	5) _____
6) _____	6) _____
7) _____	7) _____
8) _____	8) _____
9) _____	9) _____
10) _____	10) _____
11) _____	11) _____
12) _____	12) _____
13) _____	13) _____
14) _____	14) _____
15) _____	15) _____
16) _____	
17) _____	

133. BASKETBALL ARENAS

Match the present-day teams with the arenas in which they play. In some cases the first part of the proper noun has been omitted in order to protect the identification of the site.

1) __ Atlanta
2) __ Boston
3) __ Chicago
4) __ Cleveland
5) __ Dallas
6) __ Denver
7) __ Detroit
8) __ Golden State
9) __ Houston
10) __ Indiana
11) __ Kansas City
12) __ Los Angeles
13) __ Milwaukee
14) __ New Jersey
15) __ New York
16) __ Philadelphia
17) __ Phoenix
18) __ Portland
19) __ San Antonio
20) __ San Diego
21) __ Seattle
22) __ Utah
23) __ Washington

a) Kingdome
b) _____ Garden
c) Capital Centre
d) The Omni
e) Salt Palace
f) The Summit
g) The Forum
h) _____ Arena
i) _____ Stadium
j) The Spectrum
k) _____ Coliseum
l) Veterans' Memorial Coliseum
m) HemisFair Arena
n) Madison Square Garden
o) Market Square Arena
p) _____ Sports Arena
q) The Coliseum
r) Brendan Byrne Arena
s) Kemper Arena
t) McNichols Sports Arena
u) Memorial Coliseum
v) Pontiac Silverdome
w) Reunion Arena

134. SEATING SPACE

Are the listed arenas over or under 17,000 in seating space? Write either "Over" or "Under."

1) _____ The Omni
2) _____ Boston Garden
3) _____ Chicago Stadium
4) _____ Richfield Coliseum
5) _____ Reunion Arena
6) _____ McNichols Sports Arena
7) _____ Pontiac Silverdome
8) _____ Oakland Coliseum
9) _____ The Summit
10) _____ Market Square Arena
11) _____ Kemper Arena
12) _____ The Forum
13) _____ Milwaukee Arena
14) _____ Brendan Byrne Arena
15) _____ Madison Square Garden
16) _____ The Spectrum
17) _____ Arizona Veterans' Memorial Coliseum
18) _____ (Portland) Memorial Coliseum
19) _____ HemisFair Arena
20) _____ San Diego Sports Arena
21) _____ The Kingdome
22) _____ The Salt Palace
23) _____ Capital Centre

135. FATHERS AND SONS

We'll give you the father's first name; you give us the son's first name.

1) *Matt*	Guokas	_____
2) *Dolph*	Schayes	_____
3) *Jim*	Paxson	_____
4) *Bill*	Van Breda Kolff	_____

136. BROTHER COMBOS

We'll provide you with the brothers' first names; you provide us with their last name. We slipped some retired players into the list.

1) Bernard and Al _____
2) Major and Caldwell _____
3) Ray and Gus _____
4) James and Keith _____
5) Dick and Al _____
6) George and Ed _____
7) Don and Mac _____
8) Sam and Tom _____
9) Dick and Tom _____

137. FOREIGN TALENT

Match the players with the foreign countries or islands where they were born.

1) __ Karl Gudmundsson   a) Bahamas
2) __ James Lee Donaldson   b) Iceland
3) __ Ernest Grunfeld   c) Germany
4) __ Swen Nater   d) Romania
5) __ Mychal Thompson   e) England
6) __ Kiki Vandeweghe   f) Netherlands

138. WEST OF EUROPE

The listed players performed, at one time or another, either in the Western League (America) or in Europe. Write next to their names either "W" for Western League or "E" for Europe.

1) Mel Bennett __   11) Gerald Henderson __
2) Marvin Barnes __   12) George Johnson __
3) Art Collins __   13) Myles Patrick __
4) Jeff Cook __   14) Abdul Jeelani __
5) Brad Davis __   15) Bill Laimbeer __
6) Geoff Crompton __   16) Jackie Robinson __
7) Coby Dietrick __   17) Tom McMillen __
8) James Lee Donaldson __ 18) Willie Smith __
9) Mike Evans __   19) John Roche __
10) Eric Fernsten __   20) Jeff Wilkens __

139. COACHES OF THE YEAR

There have been 18 different Coaches of the Year since the award was first instituted in 1963. Only two coaches have repeated. Both of them won it with different teams. Hence 20 answers are needed. Can you provide them?

1) Boston   _____ (1965)
2) Boston   _____ (1973)
3) Boston   _____ (1980)
4) St. Louis   _____ (1963)
5) St. Louis   _____ (1968)
6) Chicago   _____ (1967)
7) Chicago   _____ (1971)
8) San Francisco   _____ (1964)
9) Philadelphia   _____ (1966)
10) Baltimore   _____ (1969)
11) New York   _____ (1970)
12) Los Angeles   _____ (1972)
13) Detroit   _____ (1974)
14) Kansas City-Omaha _____ (1975)
15) Cleveland   _____ (1976)
16) Houston   _____ (1977)
17) Atlanta   _____ (1978)
18) Kansas City   _____ (1979)
19) Indiana   _____ (1981)

140. WINNING(?) COACHES

Did (do) the listed coaches have winning or losing records in the NBA? If you think they were (are) on the positive side of the ledger, write a "W" next to their names; if you think they were (are) on the negative side of the ledger, write an "L" next to their names. The records are up-to-date through the 1981 season.

1) Red Auerbach ___
2) Paul Westhead ___
3) Joe Mullaney ___
4) Les Harrison ___
5) Dolph Schayes ___
6) Phil Johnson ___
7) Larry Costello ___
8) Bob Cousy ___
9) Johnny Egan ___
10) Dick McGuire ___
11) Buddy Jeannette ___
12) John Kundla ___
13) Charles Wolf ___
14) Al Cervi ___
15) Jack McMahon ___
16) Red Holzman ___
17) Bill Russell ___
18) Fuzzy Levane ___
19) Harry Gallatin ___
20) Kevin Loughery ___
21) Cotton Fitzsimmons ___
22) John MacLeod ___
23) Larry Brown ___
24) Paul Birch ___
25) George Senesky ___

26) Jack Ramsay ___
27) Doug Moe ___
28) K.C. Jones ___
29) Hubie Brown ___
30) Billy Cunningham ___
31) Gene Shue ___
32) Dick Motta ___
33) Eddie Gottlieb ___
34) Paul Seymour ___
35) Bill van Breda Kolff ___
36) Tom Heinsohn ___
37) Lenny Wilkens ___
38) Jerry West ___
39) Ray Scott ___
40) Charlie Eckman ___
41) Al Attles ___
42) Alex Hannum ___
43) Bill Sharman ___
44) Fred Schaus ___
45) Bill Fitch ___
46) Tom Nissalke ___
47) Bob Leonard ___
48) Don Nelson ___
49) Richie Guerin ___
50) Joe Lapchick ___

141. COACHING CHAMPIONSHIPS

Of the following coaches put the multiple league winners in the left-hand column and the one-time league winners in the right-hand column: Les Harrison, Dick Motta, Alex Hannum, Eddie Gottlieb, Red Auerbach, Kevin Loughery, Buddy Jeannette, Jack Ramsay, John Kundla, Al Cervi, Bob Leonard, Al Attles, Tom Heinsohn, Red Holzman, Bill Sharman, George Senesky, Larry Costello, and Bill Russell. ABA championships count. The order is not important.

Multiple Champs
1) _____
2) _____
3) _____
4) _____
5) _____
6) _____
7) _____
8) _____
9) _____

One-Time Champs
1) _____
2) _____
3) _____
4) _____
5) _____
6) _____
7) _____
8) _____
9) _____

Flash Followup

1) _____ Which coach won a record nine titles?
2) _____ Which player-coach won back-to-back titles?
3) _____ Which coach won a record three titles in the ABA?
4) _____ Which coach won two titles in the ABA?
5) _____ Which coach won his five crowns within a span of six years?

171

6) _____ Which coach won championships with three different teams?
7) _____ Which coach won one title in the NBA and one title in the ABA?
8) _____ Which one-time winner was a player-coach?

142. NEW YORK KNICK HEAD COACHES

How many of the Knicks' ten head coaches can you name? Respective dates are provided in order to put the total coaching picture into perspective.

1) _____ (1946–47)
2) _____ (1947–56)
3) _____ (1956–58)
4) _____ (1958–60)
5) _____ (1960–61)
6) _____ (1961–65)
7) _____ (1965–66)
8) _____ (1966–68)
9) _____ (1968–77 and 1979–   )
10) _____ (1977–78)

143. BOSTON CELTIC HEAD COACHES

How many of the 8 can you name?

1) _____ (1946–48)
2) _____ (1948–50)
3) _____ (1950–66)
4) _____ (1966–69)
5) _____ (1969–78)
6) _____ (1978)
7) _____ (1978–79)
8) _____ (1979–)

144. MINNEAPOLIS-LOS ANGELES LAKER HEAD COACHES

How many of the 12 can you name?

1) _____ (1948–59)
2) _____ (1957–58)
3) _____ (1959–60)
4) _____ (1960)
5) _____ (1960–67)
6) _____ (1967–69)
7) _____ (1969–71)
8) _____ (1971–76)
9) _____ (1976–79)
10) _____ (1979)
11) _____ (1980–81)
12) _____ (1981–)

145. THE PHILADELPHIA-SAN FRANCISCO-GOLDEN STATE WARRIOR HEAD COACHES

How many of the 11 can you name?

1) _____ (1946–55)
2) _____ (1955–58)
3) _____ (1958–59)
4) _____ (1959–61)
5) _____ (1961–62)
6) _____ (1962–63)

7) _____ (1963–66)
8) _____ (1966–68)
9) _____ (1968–70)
10) _____ (1970–80 and

11) _____ (1980)

146. THE SYRACUSE NATIONAL-PHILADELPHIA 76ER HEAD COACHES

How many of the 9 can you name?

1) _____ (1949–56)
2) _____ (1956–60)
3) _____ (1960–63 and 1966–68)
4) _____ (1963–66)
5) _____ (1968–72)
6) _____ (1972–73)
7) _____ (1973)
8) _____ (1973–77)
9) _____ (1977–   )

147. ORIGINAL COACHES: PART I

Are you sitting back? Resting on your laurels? Wondering about the competition? Well, the opponents that you're going to run into in the following series of quizzes are guaranteed to send you into a slow-down offense. But, then again, maybe you'll beat the press.

Match the coaches in the left-hand column with the teams in the right-hand column that were original franchises or original team-name changes.

1) ___ Howie Schultz   a) St. Louis Hawks
2) ___ Richie Guerin   b) Milwaukee Hawks
3) ___ Bill Fitch   c) Anderson Packers
4) ___ Dixie Moore   d) Chicago Bulls
5) ___ John Kerr   e) Cleveland Rebels
6) ___ Harold Olsen   f) Tri-Cities Blackhawks
7) ___ Roger Potter   g) Baltimore Bullets
8) ___ Honey Russell   h) Chicago Stags
9) ___ Red Holzman   i) Atlanta Hawks
10) ___ Buddy Jeannette   j) Cleveland Cavaliers
11) ___ Dutch Dehnert   k) Denver Nuggets
12) ___ Bob Bass   l) Denver Nuggets
13) ___ James Darden   (ABA-NBA)
                           m) Boston Celtics

148. ORIGINAL COACHES: PART II

Match the coaches in the left-hand column with the teams in the right-hand column that were original franchises or original team-name changes.

1) ___ Jack McMahon
2) ___ Cliff Barker
3) ___ Bobby Wanzer
4) ___ Glen Curtis
5) ___ Bob Feerick
6) ___ Carl Bennett
7) ___ Bob Cousy
8) ___ John Givens
9) ___ Charlie Eckman
10) ___ Larry Staverman
11) ___ Les Harrison
12) ___ Bruce Hale
13) ___ Eddie Gottlieb

a) Detroit Falcons
b) Indianapolis Olympians
c) Rochester Royals
d) Cincinnati Royals
e) Kentucky Colonels
f) Fort Wayne Pistons
g) San Diego Rockets
h) Indianapolis Jets
i) Philadelphia Warriors
j) Indiana Pacers
k) Golden State Warriors
l) Detroit Pistons
m) Kansas City Kings

149. ORIGINAL COACHES: PART III

Match the coaches in the left-hand column with the teams in the right-hand column that were original franchises or original team-name changes.

1) __ John Kundla
2) __ Fred Schaus
3) __ Tex Winter
4) __ Babe McCarthy
5) __ Bob Bass
6) __ Joe Mullaney
7) __ Jim Pollard
8) __ Larry Costello
9) __ Max Zaslofsky
10) __ Kevin Loughery
11) __ Neil Cohalan
12) __ Al Cervi
13) __ Dolph Schayes

a) Minnesota Muskies
b) Philadelphia 76ers
c) Minneapolis Lakers
d) Syracuse Nats
e) Milwaukee Bucks
f) New Jersey Nets
g) New York Knicks
h) New Jersey Americans
i) Houston Rockets
j) Memphis Tams
k) Los Angeles Lakers
l) New Orleans Buc-
    caneers
m) Memphis Sounds

150. ORIGINAL COACHES:
PART IV

Match the coaches in the left-hand column with the teams in the right-hand column that were original franchises or original team-name changes.

1) ___ John Kerr
2) ___ Vince Cazetta
3) ___ Jim Harding
4) ___ John Clark
5) ___ Jack McMahon
6) ___ Paul Birch
7) ___ Rolland Todd
8) ___ Robert Morris
9) ___ Ken Loeffler
10) ___ Slater Martin
11) ___ Bones McKinney
12) ___ Larry Brown
13) ___ Cliff Hagan

a) Portland Trail Blazers
b) Dallas Chapparrals
c) Pittsburgh Condors
d) Pittsburgh Pipers II
e) Phoenix Suns
f) Minnesota Pipers
g) Pittsburgh Pipers I
h) Pittsburgh Ironmen
i) Providence Steamrollers
j) Carolina Cougars
k) St. Louis Spirits
l) St. Louis Bombers
m) Houston Mavericks

151. ORIGINAL COACHES: PART V

Match the coaches in the left-hand column with the teams in the right-hand column that were original franchises or original team-name changes.

1) __ Max Williams
2) __ Tom Nissalke
3) __ Dolph Schayes
4) __ Gene Shue
5) __ K.C. Jones
6) __ Bill Musselman
7) __ Al Bianchi
8) __ Ken Suesens
9) __ Ed Sadowski
10) __ Bill Sharman
11) __ Scotty Robertson
12) __ Al Brightman

a) Seattle SuperSonics
b) Toronto Huskies
c) San Diego Clippers
d) Texas Chapparrals
e) Anaheim Amigos
f) Los Angeles Stars
g) San Antonio Spurs
h) San Diego Sails
i) New Orleans Jazz
j) San Diego Conquista-
dors
k) Buffalo Braves
l) Sheboygan Redskins

152. ORIGINAL COACHES: PART VI

Match the coaches in the left-hand column with the teams in the right-hand column that were original franchises or original team-name changes. In this quiz K.C. Jones and Al Bianchi may be used twice.

1) __ Tom Nissalke
2) __ Bill Sharman
3) __ Bruce Hale
4) __ Al Bianchi
5) __ Al Bianchi
6) __ Jim Pollard
7) __ Jack McMahon
8) __ Bob Leonard
9) __ K.C. Jones
10) __ K.C. Jones
11) __ Red Auerbach
12) __ Charles Shipp

a) Waterloo Hawks
b) Virginia Squires
c) Washington Bullets
d) Washington Capitols (ABA)
e) Utah Stars
f) Chicago Zephyrs
g) Capital Bullets
h) Oakland Oaks
i) Chicago Packers
j) Utah Jazz
k) Baltimore Bullets
l) Washington Capitols

153. 60-WIN SEASONS

All of the mentors listed below have guided their clubs to 50-or-more-win seasons at least once during their pro coaching careers. However, can you zero in on the 14 members of this select group who have led pro teams to 60-or-more-win seasons?

Paul Seymour
Richie Guerin
Red Auerbach
Bill Russell
Tom Heinsohn
Bill Fitch
Dick Motta
Larry Brown
Ray Scott
Al Attles
Bob Leonard
Les Harrison
Jack McMahon
Joe Mullaney
Babe McCarthy
Hubie Brown
John Kundla
Fred Schaus
Bill van Breda Kolff
Bill Sharman
Al Bianchi

Jerry West
Paul Westhead
Jim Pollard
Larry Costello
Don Nelson
Kevin Loughery
Red Holzman
Al Cervi
Dolph Schayes
Alex Hannum
Jack Ramsay
Gene Shue
Billy Cunningham
John MacLeod
Vince Cazetta
Bob Bass
Doug Moe
Stan Albeck
Len Wilkens
LaDell Anderson
K.C. Jones

1) _____
2) _____
3) _____
4) _____
5) _____
6) _____
7) _____

8) _____
9) _____
10) _____
11) _____
12) _____
13) _____
14) _____

154. ONCE IS ENOUGH

Seven of the 14 coaches who are listed in the answers to the preceding quiz have won 60-or-more games in a season *only* once. Which ones?

1) _____   5) _____
2) _____   6) _____
3) _____   7) _____
4) _____

155. ONCE IS NOT ENOUGH

Five of the 14 coaches who are listed in the answers to Quiz 153 "60-Win Seasons" have won 60-or-more games in a season twice. Which ones?

1) _____   4) _____
2) _____   5) _____
3) _____

156. TWICE IS NOT ENOUGH

Two of the 14 coaches who are listed in the answers to Quiz 153 "60-Win Seasons" have won 60-or-more games in a season a record three times. Which ones?

1) _____   2) _____

157. COACH'S WHO'S WHO

Refer to the 14 coaches listed in the answers to Quiz
153, "60-Win Seasons," to fill in the blanks to the following questions.

1) _____ Who led his team to a league-record 69
wins?

2) _____ Who guided a 68–13 club?

3) _____ Who has been the only coach to win 60 or
more games with two different teams?

4) _____ Who won more than 60 games in 1979–80
and 1980–81?

5) _____ Who in 1980–81 won 60 games for the first
time?

6) _____ Who, in addition to winning 60 or more
games twice, guided teams with 50 or more wins six times?

7) _____ Who coached his team to two NBA titles in
his last two years as a player?

8) _____ Who averaged 59 wins a season from 1971–
72 to 1975–76?

9) _____ Who had a 68–14 season with the Celtics?

10) _____ Who amassed a 68–16 mark with the 1971–
72 Kentucky Colonels?

11) _____ Who was the coach who led the Denver
Nuggets to back-to-back seasons of 65 and 60 wins?

12) _____ Who was the two-time 60–game winner
with one team who led the Utah Stars to a 57–win season?

13) _____ Who guided a club to three consecutive
60 or more win seasons?

14) _____ Who is the present-day coach who averaged
56 wins a season from 1977–78 to 1980–81?

15) _____ Who averaged 54 wins a season from 1968–
69 to 1972–73?

16) _____ Who has been the only coach of the Utah Stars to win 60 games in a season?

17) _____ Who, in his three full seasons with the Washington Bullets, averaged 52 wins a season?

158. 50-WIN SEASONS

Twenty-eight of the 42 coaches listed in Quiz 153 "60-Win Seasons" never won 60 games in a year, but they did win 50 or more contests in a campaign. We're going to zero in on the 11 coaches who did it two or more times. The number of coaches who won 50 or more games "two," "three," "four," or "five" times are designated beneath each category. The order of names may vary.

Two Times
1) _____
2) _____
3) _____
4) _____
5) _____

Three Times
1) _____
2) _____
3) _____
4) _____

Four Times
1) _____

Five Times
1) _____

159. GREAT GAMES

Match the following players with the most points that they ever scored in a regulation game: Jerry West, Elgin Baylor, Wilt Chamberlain, Rick Barry, George Mikan, George Gervin, Pete Maravich, Joe Fulks, and David Thompson. The above players are the only ones in the history of pro basketball to score more than 60 points in a game.

1) _____ (100)
2) _____ (73)
3) _____ (71)
4) _____ (68)
5) _____ (64)
6) _____ (63)
7) _____ (63)
8) _____ (63)
9) _____ (61)

Flash Followup

10) _____ Who scored 60 or more points a record 32 times?

160. CHAMPIONSHIP SWEEPS

Three teams in the history of the NBA championship series have swept their opponents. How many of them can you name?

1) _____
2) _____
3) _____

161. ROOKIES OF THE YEAR

Match the following ten rookies with the years in which they won the Rookie of the Year Award: Phil Ford, Buck

Williams, Bob McAdoo, Adrian Dantley, Walter Davis, Larry Bird, Darrell Griffith, Ernie Di Gregorio, Alvan Adams, and Keith Wilkes. Teams are provided.

1) 1972–73 _____ Buffalo
2) 1973–74 _____ Buffalo
3) 1974–75 _____ Golden State
4) 1975–76 _____ Phoenix
5) 1976–77 _____ Buffalo
6) 1977–78 _____ Phoenix
7) 1978–79 _____ Kansas City
8) 1979–80 _____ Boston
9) 1980–81 _____ Utah
10) 1981–82 _____ New Jersey

162. 1982 COLLEGE DRAFT

Match the teams in the left-hand column with the players in the right-hand column whom they picked first in the 1982 draft. Some teams didn't get a pick in the first or second round. We're still interested in their first pick. Some teams had two first-round picks. Zero in on their first choice.

1) __ Hawks   a) Paul Pressey
2) __ Celtics   b) Lafayette Lever
3) __ Bulls   c) Keith Edmonson
4) __ Cavaliers   d) Lester Conner
5) __ Mavericks   e) Sleepy Floyd
6) __ Nuggets   f) Terry Cummings
7) __ Pistons   g) Darren Tillis
8) __ Warriors   h) Bryan Warrick
9) __ Rockets   i) David Thirdkill
10) __ Pacers   j) John Bagley
11) __ Kings   k) Terry Teagle
12) __ Lakers   l) Dominique Wilkins

13) __ Bucks	m) Mark McNamara
14) __ Nets	n) Quintin Dailey
15) __ Knicks	o) Trent Tucker
16) __ 76ers	p) Oliver Robinson
17) __ Suns	q) John Greig
18) __ Blazers	r) Bill Garnett
19) __ Spurs	s) James Worthy
20) __ Clippers	t) LaSalle Thompon
21) __ Sonics	u) Cliff Levingston
22) __ Jazz	v) Rob Williams
23) __ Bullets	w) Clark Kellogg

163. 1981-82 STAT LEADERS

Fill in the blanks.

1) _____ Who led the league in scoring with a 32.3 game average?

2) _____ Who led the league in field goal percentage with a .652 success rate? In 1980–81 he shot .670 from the floor.

3) _____ Who led the league in game rebounds by pulling down 14.7 per contest? It's the third time he's done it.

4) _____ Who led all shooters from the charity-stripe line with an .899 percentage? Believe it or not, he shot .899 in 1980–81, his rookie year, too.

5) _____ Who led the league in blocked shots for the second year in a row with 3.12 per game? He's won three individual honors in this category.

6) _____ Who led the league in assists with 9.6 per game? He did it in his second pro season.

7) _____ Who averaged a league-leading 2.67 steals per game? Last year he averaged 3.43 to lead the league in his rookie year.

8) _____ Who paced the NBA's long-range gunners with a .439 mark in 3-point field goal shooting percentage? He plays in New York.

164. MEN AT THE MIKE

Match the former NBA players in the left-hand column with the teams for which they presently announce games on television, radio, or both, in the right-hand column.

___ 1) Bob Cousy   a) Bucks
___ 2) Johnny Kerr   b) Jazz
___ 3) Gus Johnson   c) Celtics
___ 4) Keith Erickson   d) 76ers
___ 5) Jon McGlocklin   e) Nets
___ 6) Dick Van Arsdale   f) Bulls
___ 7) Hot Rod Hundley   g) Lakers
___ 8) Phil Jackson   h) Cavaliers
___ 9) Matt Guokas   i) Suns

VICTORY THROUGH DEFEAT

No one would ever call Jerry West a loser.

They called him "Mr. Clutch." When the pressure was at its peak, West was at his best. In 13 playoff-performing seasons he scored a record 4,457 points and averaged an all-time runner-up 29.1 points a game.

Yet he perennially played on teams that ended up runners-up. In his first ten playoff appearances, his teams gained the finals seven times. Each time the Lakers lost.

Often they came close. The 1968–69 championship series bears out the type of reward West got for his efforts. The Lakers, who won in the West, lost to the Celtics, who finished fourth in the East. West had averaged a playoff record 40.6 points a game in 1964–65. But his performance in the championship series of 1968–69 was undoubtedly his best. In his first five games he scored 53, 41, 24, 40, and 39 points, respectively.

In Game Five, however, he pulled a hamstring muscle; he was neutralized by his handicap in Game Six. But in Game Seven West rose above his injury and was once again his brilliant self.

At one point in the fourth period, the Celtics were leading by 17 points. But West reached deep within himself and came up with an unbelievable effort that just fell short. In the final minutes he scored 14 of the Lakers' final 19 points. In addition, he dove all over the court and constantly came up with timely steals and assists.

But in the end the Celtics, led by John Havlicek, held off the Lakers' surge, 108–106. West's gallant effort—42 points and 12 assists—was just not enough. But he was no loser. He was a winner—in defeat.

The Celtics showed heart in that series, too. They knew that player-coach Bill Russell was calling it a career after playing on a record 11 championship teams in 13 years. They wanted him to go out on top—and he did!

Another Celtic great retired after that championship season, too, a great who had compiled a regular-season career scoring average of 17.7 and a playoff mark of 18.9. At one point in his playoff career, he averaged over 20 points a game in seven consecutive years.

You might say that "Mr. Inside" and "Mr. Outside" retired the Celtic dynasty with themselves.

Who was "Mr. Outside?"

Answer: Sam Jones

FOURTH-PERIOD SCORE

(Total just the fourth-period points.)

Points
You __ The NBA __
Games
You __ The NBA __

ANSWERS

THE FIRST QUARTER

1. Today in the NBA

1) John Drew
2) John Drew
3) Dan Roundfield
4) Eddie Johnson
5) Charlie Criss (5–8)
6) Tom McMillen
7) Bill Bradley
8) Larry Bird
9) Robert Parish
10) Cedric Maxwell
11) Kevin McHale
12) Cedric Maxwell
13) Nate Archibald
14) Rick Robey
15) Chris Ford
16) M. L. Carr
17) Artis Gilmore (.577)
18) Reggie Theus
19) Reggie Theus
20) David Greenwood
21) Larry Kenon
22) Mike Mitchell
23) Larry Kenon
24) Kenny Carr
25) Roger Phegley
26) Geoff Huston
27) Bill Laimbeer
28) James Edwards

29) James Silas
30) Jim Spanarkel
31) Tom Lagarde
32) Brad Davis
33) Bill Robinzine
34) Abdul Jeelani
35) David Thompson
36) Dan Issel
37) David Thompson
38) Alex English
39) Calvin Murphy
40) T. R. Dunn
41) John Roche
42) John Long
43) Kent Benson
44) Terry Tyler
45) Paul Mokeski
46) Ron Lee
47) World B. Free
48) Bernard King
49) Ernie Grunfeld
50) Joe Hassett
51) Mike Gale
52) John Lucas
53) Moses Malone
54) Elvin Hayes
55) Calvin Murphy
56) Robert Reid

57)	Tom Henderson	96)	Michael Ray Richard-son
58)	Major Jones		
59)	Marvin Webster	97)	Ray Williams
60)	Billy Knight	98)	Michael Ray Richard-son
61)	Mike Bantom		
62)	Mike Bantom	99)	Sly Williams
63)	George McGinnis	100)	Mike Newlin
64)	Louis Orr	101)	Campy Russell
65)	George McGinnis	102)	Mike Glenn
66)	Tom Owens	103)	Marvin Webster
67)	Dan Issel	104)	Randy Smith
68)	Don Buse	105)	Julius Erving
69)	Phil Ford	106)	Darryl Dawkins
70)	Cliff Robinson	107)	Bobby Jones
71)	Sam Lacey	108)	Andrew Toney
72)	Ernie Grunfeld	109)	Bobby Jones
73)	Leon Douglas	110)	Maurice Cheeks
74)	John Lambert	111)	Steve Mix
75)	Lloyd Walton	112)	Steve Mix
76)	Kareem Abdul-Jabbar	113)	Lionel Hollins
77)	Kareem Abdul-Jabbar	114)	Caldwell Jones
78)	Magic Johnson	115)	Dennis Johnson
79)	Norm Nixon	116)	Walter Davis
80)	Jamaal Wilkes	117)	Dennis Johnson
81)	Eddie Jordan	118)	Alvan Adams
82)	Mitch Kupchak	119)	Truck Robinson
83)	Marques Johnson	120)	Jeff Cook
84)	Bob Lanier	121)	Kyle Macy
85)	Junior Bridgeman	122)	Rich Kelley
86)	Quinn Buckner	123)	Kelvin Ransey
87)	Mickey Johnson	124)	Mychal Thompson
88)	Brian Winters (.847)	125)	Calvin Natt
89)	Harvey Catchings	126)	Billy Ray Bates
90)	Otis Birdsong	127)	Bob Gross
91)	Maurice Lucas	128)	Dave Twardzik
92)	Darwin Cook	129)	Mark Olberding
93)	Bob McAdoo	130)	George Johnson
94)	Bob McAdoo	131)	Paul Griffin (164)
95)	Bill Cartwright	132)	Dave Corzine

133) Johnny Moore	144) Bill Hanzlik
134) Johnny Moore	145) Lonnie Shelton
135) Swen Nater	146) Wally Walker
136) Phil Smith	147) Paul Westphal
137) Freeman Williams	148) Adrian Dantley
138) Brian Taylor	149) Darrell Griffith
139) Garfield Heard	150) Allan Bristow
140) Jack Sikma	151) Greg Ballard
141) John Johnson	152) Kevin Grevey
142) James Bailey	153) Jim Chones
143) Fred Brown	154) Rick Mahorn

2. The NBA in Capital Letters

The Knicks
1) Michael Ray Richardson
2) Randy Smith
3) Bill Cartwright
4) Maurice Lucas
5) Campy Russell

The 76ers
1) Maurice Cheeks
2) Lionel Hollins
3) Darryl Dawkins
4) Julius Erving
5) Caldwell Jones

The Celtics
1) Nate Archibald
2) Chris Ford
3) Robert Parish
4) Larry Bird
5) Cedric Maxwell

The Nets
1) Otis Birdsong
2) Ray Williams
3) Buck Williams
4) Mike O'Koren
5) James Bailey

The Bullets
1) Kevin Grevey
2) John Lucas
3) Rick Mahorn
4) Greg Ballard
5) Jim Chones

The Pistons
1) Isiah Thomas
2) John Long
3) Kent Benson
4) Kelly Tripucka
5) Terry Tyler

The Bulls
1) Ronnie Lester
2) Reggie Theus
3) Artis Gilmore
4) James Wilkes
5) David Greenwood

The Bucks
1) Quinn Buckner
2) Sidney Moncrief
3) Bob Lanier
4) Marques Johnson or Mickey Johnson
5) Marques Johnson or Mickey Johnson

The Hawks
1) Eddie Johnson
2) Rory Sparrow
3) Wayne Rollins
4) John Drew
5) Dan Roundfield

The Pacers
1) Don Buse
2) Johnny Davis
3) Herb Williams
4) Louis Orr
5) Billy Knight

The Cavaliers
1) Geoff Huston
2) Bobby Wilkerson
3) James Edwards
4) Kenny Carr
5) Richard Washington

The Spurs
1) George Gervin
2) Johnny Moore
3) Dave Corzine
4) Mike Mitchell
5) Mark Olberding

The Rockets
1) Calvin Murphy
2) Mike Dunleavy
3) Moses Malone
4) Elvin Hayes
5) Robert Reid

The Nuggets
1) David Thompson
2) Theodore Roosevelt Dunn
3) Dan Issel
4) Alex English
5) Kiki Vandeweghe

The Kings
1) Phil Ford
2) Mike Woodson
3) Leon Douglas
4) Reggie King
5) John Lambert

The Jazz
1) Darrell Griffith
2) Rickey Green
3) Ben Poquette
4) Adrian Dantley
5) Allan Bristow

The Mavericks
1) Jim Spanarkel
2) Rolando Blackman
3) Tom Lagarde
4) Mark Aguirre
5) Bill Robinzine

The Suns
1) Dennis Johnson
2) Walter Davis
3) Alvan Adams
4) Leonard Robinson
5) Jeff Cook

The Blazers
1) Jim Paxson
2) Kelvin Ransey
3) Mychal Thompson
4) Calvin Natt
5) Bob Gross

The Lakers
1) Magic Johnson
2) Norm Nixon
3) Kareem Abdul-Jabbar
4) Jamaal Wilkes
5) Mitch Kupchak

The SuperSonics
1) Fred Brown
2) Gus Williams

3) Jack Sikma
4) Lonnie Shelton
5) Danny Vranes

The Warriors
1) Lloyd Free
2) Purvis Short
3) Joe Barry Carroll
4) Bernard King
5) Larry Smith

The Clippers
1) Phil Smith
2) Brian Taylor
3) Swen Nater
4) Michael Brooks
5) Joe Bryant

3. Season Assist Leaders

1) Lenny Wilkens
2) Bob Cousy
3) Guy Rodgers
4) Lenny Wilkens
5) Brad Davis
6) Al Smith
7) Kevin Porter
8) Guy Rodgers
9) John Lucas
10) Don Buse
11) Nate Archibald
12) Jerry West

13) Oscar Robertson
14) Kevin Porter
15) Michael Richardson
16) Wilt Chamberlain
17) Gail Goodrich
18) Kelvin Ransey
19) Mike Gale
20) Ernie Di Gregorio
21) Lenny Wilkens
22) Pete Maravich
23) Kevin Porter

4. Season Rebound Leaders

1) Bob Pettit
2) Bill Russell

3) Tom Boerwinkle
4) Jim Brewer

5) Tom Lagarde
6) Spencer Haywood
7) Bob Lanier
8) Wilt Chamberlain
9) Moses Malone
10) Mel Daniels
11) Jerry Lucas
12) Wilt Chamberlain
13) Kareem Abdul-Jabbar
14) Billy Paultz

15) Willis Reed
16) Wilt Chamberlain
17) Paul Silas
18) Lloyd Neal
19) Swen Nater
20) Elmore Smith
21) Spencer Haywood
22) Len Robinson
23) Walt Bellamy

5. Season Scoring Leaders

1) Bob Pettit
2) John Havlicek
3) Bob Love
4) Mike Mitchell
5) Jim Spanarkel
6) Spencer Haywood
7) Dave Bing
8) Wilt Chamberlain
9) Elvin Hayes
10) George McGinnis
11) Nate Archibald
12) Elgin Baylor

13) Kareem Abdul-Jabbar
14) Rick Barry
15) Richie Guerin
16) Wilt Chamberlain
17) Charlie Scott
18) Geoff Petrie
19) George Gervin
20) Bob McAdoo
21) Spencer Haywood
22) Adrian Dantley
23) Walt Bellamy

6. Career Highs

1) Abdul-Jabbar (55)
2) Archibald (55)
3) (Fred) Brown (58)
4) Chenier (53)
5) Dantley (55)
6) Drew (50)
7) Gervin (63)
8) Hayes (54)
9) Kenon (51)
10) (Bernard) King (50)

11) Knight (52)
12) Malone (53)
13) McAdoo (52)
14) Murphy (57)
15) Newlin (52)
16) (Len) Robinson (51)
17) (Phil) Smith (51)
18) (David) Thompson (73)
19) (Fred) Williams (51)

7. Playoff Highs

1) Abdul-Jabbar (46)
2) (Fred) Brown (45)
3) Erving (40)
4) Gervin (46)
5) Grevey (41)
6) Hayes (46)
7) Hollins (55)
8) (Magic) Johnson (42)
9) Malone (42)
10) McAdoo (50)
11) Murphy (42)
12) (David) Thompson (40)
13) (Mychal) Thompson (40)

8. .500 Career Shooters?

1) Abdul-Jabbar
2) Birdsong
3) Dantley
4) Davis
5) Davis
6) Dawkins
7) Erving
8) Gilmore
9) Gross
10) Johnson
11) Jones
12) King
13) Knight
14) Kupchak
15) Lanier
16) Malone
17) Maxwell
18) Nixon
19) Owens
20) Westphal
21) Nater
22) Gervin
23) Rollins
24) Parish
25) Ray

9. Sub-20-Point-a-Game Scorers

1) Adams
2) Bridgeman
3) Ford
4) Hollins
5) (Dennis) Johnson
6) (Eddie) Johnson
7) (Mickey) Johnson
8) Long
9) Nater
10) Paultz
11) Robisch
12) Roundfield
13) Taylor
14) Wedman
15) Winters

10. 20-Point (Season) Playoff Averages

1) Abdul-Jabbar (30.3)
2) Bates (26.7)
3) Bird (21.7)
4) Burleson (20.7)
5) Collins (21.5)
6) Dandridge (20.1)
7) Davis (20.6)
8) Erving (24.6)
9) Gervin (29.3)
10) Hayes (23.1)

11) Issel (21.2)

12) (Marques) Johnson (23.0)
13) (Bernard) King (26.0)
14) Lanier (22.8)
15) Malone (24.2)
16) McAdoo (30.3)
17) (David) Thompson (25.5)
18) (Mychal) Thompson (25.0)
19) Westphal (21.5)
20) Williamson (21.5)

11. 25-Point-Plus Scorers

1) Abdul-Jabbar (26.4)
2) Bird (30.3)
3) Carr (34.6)
4) Dantley (25.8)
5) Drew (25.2)
6) Erving (26.3)
7) Gervin (26.8)
8) Hayes (31.0)
9) Issel (25.8)

10) Malone (26.1)
11) (Mickey) Johnson (26.1)
12) King (25.8)
13) Lanier (27.6)
14) McGinnis (30.0)
15) Murphy (33.1)
16) Williams (30.7)

12. Hitting the Open Man

Nate Archibald
Don Buse
Mack Calvin
Maurice Cheeks
Johnny Davis
Phil Ford
Tom Henderson
Armond Hill

Norm Nixon
Kevin Porter
Michael Ray Richardson
Randy Smith
Ricky Sobers
Reggie Theus
Wally Walker
Paul Westphal

Marques Johnson   Jo Jo White
Allen Leavell   Ray Williams
John Lucas

13. The Hackers

1) Bailey (11)   15) Meriweather (21)
2) Brown (18)   16) Owens (15)
3) Douglas (13)   17) Poquette (18)
4) Drew (19)   18) Porter (14)
5) Edwards (16)   19) Robinzine (19)
6) Gervin (12)   20) Rollins (19)
7) Hawes (13)   21) Roundfield (16)
8) Hill (15)   22) Shelton (11)
9) Hubbard (14)   23) Van Breda Kolff (11)
10) (George) Johnson (20) 24) (Kermit) Washington
11) (Mickey) Johnson (11)   (11)
12) Kunnert (17)   25) (R. L.) Washington
13) Lacey (11)   (13)
14) McGinnis (16)   26) Wicks (14)

14. 1981 College Draft

1) 1   14) 2
2) 2   15) 1
3) 2   16) 2
4) 1   17) 2
5) 1   18) 1
6) 1   19) 2
7) 2   20) 1
8) 2   21) 2
9) 1   22) 1
10) 2   23) 1
11) 2   24) 2
12) 1   25) 2
13) 1

15. High and Low

First-Round
1) Bantom
2) Whitney
3) Boynes
4) Brown
5) Corzine
6) Davis (Brad)
7) Evans
8) Hamilton
9) Lambert
10) McMillen
11) Ray
12) Sanders
13) Walker
14) Woodson

Low-Round
1) Bibby
2) Carr
3) Cook
4) Dandridge
5) (Ron) Davis
6) Dunleavy
7) Ford
8) Griffin
9) (George) Johnson
10) (Mickey) Johnson
11) McKinney
12) Mix
13) Scott
14) Smith

16. First, Second, and Down the List

First-Round
1) Abdul-Jabbar
2) Benson
3) Carr
4) Carroll
5) Collins
6) Hayes
7) (Magic) Johnson
8) Lanier
9) Lucas
10) (David) Thompson
11) (Mychal) Thompson

Second-Round
1) Barnes
2) Birdsong
3) Brewer
4) Ford
5) Greenwood
6) Griffith
7) May
8) McAdoo
9) Tomjanovich
10) Unseld
11) Wicks

Down the List
1) Boone
2) Calvin
3) Dunleavy
4) Gilmore
5) Issel

6) Leavell
7) Paultz
8) Smith
9) Williamson

17. Player Positions

1) Center	21) Guard
2) Forward	22) Forward
3) Guard	23) Center
4) Guard	24) Center
5) Center	25) Guard
6) Forward	26) Guard
7) Guard	27) Forward
8) Center	28) Center
9) Guard	29) Forward
10) Forward	30) Center
11) Forward	31) Guard
12) Center	32) Center
13) Forward	33) Guard
14) Center	34) Guard
15) Center	35) Guard
16) Center	36) Forward
17) Guard	37) Center
18) Forward	38) Forward
19) Forward	39) Forward
20) Guard	40) Forward

18. Current NBA Numbers

1) Robert Parish	14) Lionel Hollins
2) Kevin Porter	15) Don Buse
3) Phil Ford	16) Norm Nixon
4) Gus Williams	17) Abdul Jeelani
5) Alex English	18) Billy Ray Bates
6) Eddie Johnson	19) Ray Williams
7) Sidney Moncrief	20) Charlie Criss
8) Jim Paxson	21) Bob Lanier
9) Adrian Dantley	22) Scott May
10) Billy Paultz	23) Lorenzo Romar
11) Julius Erving	24) Geoff Huston
12) Nate Archibald	25) Lloyd Free
13) Marques Johnson	26) John Drew

27) Joe Bryant	42) Len Elmore
28) Moses Malone	43) Greg Ballard
29) John Long	44) Mickey Johnson
30) John Johnson	45) Jack Sikma
31) Wayne Rollins	46) Dan Issel
32) Bernard King	47) George Gervin
33) Mike O'Koren	48) Joe Meriweather
34) Dan Roundfield	49) Steve Mix
35) James Wilkes	50) Jamaal Wilkes
36) Magic Johnson	51) Artis Gilmore
37) Larry Bird	52) Darryl Dawkins
38) Kareem Abdul-Jabbar	53) Bill Robinzine
39) Jim Spanarkel	54) Tom McMillen
40) Darrell Griffith	55) Kiki Vandeweghe
41) Dave Corzine	

19. Big Trades

1) s	11) a
2) t	12) o
3) k	13) f
4) c	14) m
5) d	15) l
6) i	16) q
7) j	17) n
8) r	18) p
9) g	19) e
10) h	20) b

20. Did They or Didn't They?

Nate Archibald (1981)	Phil Smith (1975)
Henry Bibby (1973)	Rick Robey (1981)
Jack Sikma (1979)	Lonnie Shelton (1979)
Mitch Kupchak (1978)	Robert Parish (1981)
Fred Brown (1979)	Paul Westphal (1974)

Norm Nixon (1980)   Jim Chones (1980)
Elvin Hayes (1978)   Gus Williams (1979)
Bob Gross (1977)   Cornbread Maxwell (1981)
Lionel Hollins (1977)   Dennis Awtrey (1979)
Dennis Johnson (1979)

21. Last Names

1) Boynes   11) Jones
2) Bradley   12) Knight
3) Bridgeman   13) Phegley
4) Catchings   14) Richardson
5) Dietrick   15) Romar
6) Fernsten   16) Scales
7) Heard   17) Short
8) Hill   18) Terry
9) Hordges   19) Van Breda Kolff
10) Johnson   20) Williams

22. The Right Height

7-0 to 7-2   *6-8 to 6-11*
1) Artis Gilmore (7-2)   1) Jim Chones (6-11)
2) Robert Parish (7-0)   2) Elvin Hayes (6-9)
3) Kareem Abdul-Jabbar (3) Bobby Jones (6-9)
   (7-2)   4) Bob Lanier (6-11)
4) Tom Burleson (7-2)   5) Jack Sikma (6-11)
5) Bill Cartwright (7-1)   6) Dan Issel (6-9)
6) Tree Rollins (7-1)   7) Alvan Adams (6-9)
7) Marvin Webster (7-1)   8) Joe Bryant (6-9)
8) Joe Barry Carroll (7-0)   9) Steve Hawes (6-9)
9) James Edwards (7-0)   10) Campy Russell (6-8)
10) Rich Kelley (7-0)   11) Toby Knight (6-9)
11) Jeff Wilkins (7-0)   12) Phil Hubbard (6-8)
12) Paul Mokeski (7-0)

6-4 to 6-7
1) Truck Robinson (6-7)
2) Steve Mix (6-7)
3) Mike Newlin (6-4)
4) Michael Ray Richardson (6-5)
5) Allan Bristow (6-7)
6) Adrian Dantley (6-5)
7) Billy Knight (6-7)
8) John Drew (6-6)
9) Bob Dandridge (6-6)
10) Chris Ford (6-5)
11) George Gervin (6-7)
12) Darrell Griffith (6-4)

6-0 to 6-3
1) Nate Archibald (6-1)
2) Phil Ford (6-2)
3) Ed Jordan (6-1)
4) Kevin Porter (6-0)
5) Brad Davis (6-3)
6) Lloyd Free (6-1)
7) John Lucas (6-2)
8) Mike Dunleavy (6-3)
9) Maurice Cheeks (6-1)
10) Wes Matthews (6-1)
11) Johnny Davis (6-1)
12) Ken Higgs (6-0)

Under 6
1) Charlie Criss (5-8)
2) Calvin Murphy (5-9)

23. A Weighty Subject

Benson	(245)	Drollinger	(250)
Cartwright	(255)	Gminski	(250)
Corzine	(250)	Lanier	(250)
Dawkins	(251)	Mokeski	(250)
Donaldson	(270)	Paultz	(250)

24. You Be the Ref

1) R	9) R	17) R	25) R	33) R
2) P	10) R	18) P	26) R	34) P
3) P	11) P	19) P	27) P	35) P
4) R	12) P	20) R	28) P	36) R
5) R	13) R	21) R	29) R	37) R
6) P	14) P	22) P	30) P	38) R
7) R	15) P	23) P	31) P	39) P
8) P	16) R	24) R	32) P	40) P

25. Pro Potpourri

1) Artis Gilmore
2) David Greenwood
3) Bill Musselman
4) Mike Bratz
5) Dick Motta
6) Donnie Walsh
7) Nuggets
8) Nuggets
9) David Thompson, Alex English, and Dan Issel
10) Pistons
11) Bernard King
12) Larry Smith
13) Calvin Murphy
14) Moses Malone
15) James Edwards
16) Bob MacKinnon
17) Mike Newlin
18) Cliff Robinson
19) Michael Ray Richardson
20) 76ers
21) Bobby Jones
22) Billy Ray Bates
23) Julius Erving
24) Gus Williams
25) Dennis Johnson
26) Utah
27) Ricky Sobers
28) Darryl Dawkins
29) Brian Taylor
30) Mike Bratz
31) Joe Hassett
32) Artis Gilmore

THE SECOND QUARTER

26. Court Chronology I

1) Max Case
2) Walter Brown
3) Ned Irish
4) The Basketball Association of America
5) Maurice Podoloff
6) Eddie Gottlieb
7) George Mikan
8) Red Auerbach
9) Capitols
10) Joe Fulks (23.2 points a game)
11) Joe Fulks
12) John "Honey" Russell
13) 60
14) 48
15) 82
16) Philadelphia
17) Bullets
18) Chicago Gears
19) Jim Pollard
20) Max Winter

27. Court Chronology II

1) National Basketball Association
2) Ben Kerner
3) Danny Biasone
4) Harrison
5) Bob Davies
6) Indianapolis Olympians
7) Alex Groza
8) Ralph Beard
9) Chuck Cooper
10) Tri-Cities
11) Jack Molinas
12) Sol Levy
13) Chuck Cooper
14) Sweetwater Clifton
15) Charlie Share
16) Chicago
17) Max Zaslofsky
18) Andy Phillip
19) Bob Cousy
20) Ed Macauley

28. Court Chronology III

1) Dolph Schayes
2) $1,000 ($6,000 to $7,000)
3) Frank Brian
4) Paul Arizin
5) Bob Brannum
6) Bob Cousy
7) St. Louis Hawks
8) Ed Macauley
9) Cliff Hagan
10) Tom Heinsohn
11) Frank Ramsey
12) Bill Sharman
13) Maurice Stokes
14) Jack Twyman
15) Bob Pettit
16) George Mikan (42)
17) Celtics (1959)
18) Elgin Baylor
19) Eddie Gottlieb
20) Wilt Chamberlain

29. Court Chronology IV

1) Joe Lapchick
2) Wilt Chamberlain
3) Elgin Baylor
4) Wilt Chamberlain
5) Guy Rodgers
6) Walter Kennedy
7) Jack Kent Cook
8) Dave DeBusschere (Pistons)
9) Fuzzy Levane
10) Walter Brown
11) John Havlicek
12) Jerry West
13) Bill Russell (1966–67)
14) Matt Guokas
15) John Havlicek
16) Oscar Robertson (1960–61)
17) Wes Unseld (1968–69)
18) Phoenix (1969)
19) Willis Reed (1964–65)
20) Dave Stallworth

30. Court Chronology V

1) Walt Bellamy
2) Butch Komives
3) Knicks
4) Jerry West
5) Willis Reed
6) Wilt Chamberlain
7) Wilt Chamberlain (1967)
8) Bill Sharman
9) Nate Archibald (1972–73)
10) Willis Reed (1970, 1973)

11) George Mikan
12) Red, White, and Blue
13) Dick Barnett
14) John McLendon
15) Connie Hawkins
16) Abe Saperstein
17) Rick Barry
18) Pittsburgh Pipers
19) Connie Hawkins
20) Vince Cazetta

31. Court Chronology VI

1) Mel Daniels
2) Jerry Harkness
3) Jim Harding
4) Vern Mikkelsen
5) Jack Dolph
6) Lew Alcindor
7) Connie Hawkins
8) Connie Hawkins
9) Spencer Haywood
10) Artis Gilmore
11) Rick Barry
12) Billy Cunningham
13) Julius Erving
14) Wilt Chamberlain
15) Bones McKinney
16) Capitols (1946–47)
17) Hockey
18) Buddy Jeannette
19) Carl Braun
20) Joe Fulks (1946–47)

32. Court Chronology VII

1) Max Zaslofsky
2) Joe Fulks
3) Don Otten
4) Lakers
5) Syracuse Nationals
6) Bob Harrison
7) Dick McGuire
8) Tri-Cities
9) Bones McKinney
10) Bob Davies
11) Alex Groza
12) Ralph Beard
13) George Mikan
14) Six feet
15) Wilt Chamberlain
16) Bob Cousy
17) Andy Phillip (1950–51 and 1951–52)
18) Ernie Vandeweghe
19) Mel Hutchins
20) Bill Sharman

33. Court Chronology VIII

1) Bob Cousy
2) Neil Johnston
3) Dolph Schayes
4) Harry Gallatin
5) Neil Johnston (1953–55)
6) Dolph Schayes
7) George King
8) Charlie Eckman
9) Bob Pettit
10) Frank Selvy
11) Paul Arizin
12) Bob Cousy
13) Mel Hutchins
14) Bob Pettit
15) Maurice Stokes
16) Maurice Stokes (17.4)
17) Bill Russell
18) Bob Pettit
19) George Yardley (1957–58)
20) Clyde Lovellette

34. Court Chronology IX

1) Harry Gallatin
2) Bill Russell (22.7)
3) Bob Pettit (29.2)
4) Alex Groza (1949–50)
5) Bob Pettit (1956)
6) Bob Pettit (1959)
7) George Mikan
8) Elgin Baylor
9) Celtics (over the Lakers)
10) Larry Costello (1961)
11) Cliff Hagan
12) Wilt Chamberlain (1959)
13) George Mikan (Lakers)
14) Neil Johnston (Philadelphia Warriors)
15) Wilt Chamberlain (37.6)
16) Bill Russell
17) Jack Twyman (31.2)
18) Hawks (Pettit, Hagan, and Lovellette)
19) Wilt Chamberlain (1959–60)
20) Darrall Imhoff

35. Court Chronology X

1) Fred Schaus
2) Oscar Robertson (1960–61)
3) Oscar Robertson
4) Elgin Baylor (34.8)
5) Neil Johnston (1954–55)
6) Bob Pettit (1955–56)

7) Chicago Packers
8) Walt Bellamy
9) Wilt Chamberlain
10) Elgin Baylor
11) Sam Jones
12) Elgin Baylor
13) Jerry West
14) Tom Heinsohn

15) Oscar Robertson
    (11.4)
16) Wilt Chamberlain
    (44.8)
17) Guy Rodgers
18) Jerry Lucas
19) Alex Hannum
20) Bob Pettit (1960–61)

36. Court Chronology XI

1) John Havlicek
2) Bob Pettit
3) Jerry Lucas
4) Jerry Lucas
5) Wilt Chamberlain
6) Bill Russell
7) Philadelphia (1966–67)
8) Bailey Howell
9) Rick Barry
10) Dave Bing

11) Max Zaslofsky
12) Earl Monroe
13) Nate Thurmond
14) Butch van Breda Kolff
15) Ben Kerner
16) Dave DeBusschere
17) Walt Bellamy
18) Nate Archibald (6-1)
19) Bucks
20) 76ers

37. Court Chronology XII

1) Dave Cowens
2) Nate Archibald
3) Guy Rodgers
4) Larry O'Brien
5) Pete Maravich
6) Seattle
7) Kent Benson
8) Rudy Tomjanovich
9) David Thompson

10) George Gervin
11) George Gervin
12) Michael Ray Richardson
13) Rick Barry
14) 1972 Warriors
    (Mullins, Thurmond, and Cazzie Russell)

38. All-Time Greats I

1) Kareem Abdul-Jabbar
2) Sam Jones
3) Andy Phillip
4) Bob Pettit
5) Jerry West
6) Kareem Abdul-Jabbar
7) Elgin Baylor
8) Jerry West
9) Rick Barry
10) Wilt Chamberlain
11) Oscar Robertson
12) Dolph Schayes
13) Bill Sharman
14) Nate Archibald
15) Dolph Schayes
16) Nate Archibald (1972–73)
17) Dolph Schayes

39. All-Time Greats II

1) Bill Sharman
2) Lenny Wilkens
3) Jerry West
4) Bill Sharman
5) Sam Jones
6) John Havlicek
7) Earl Monroe
8) Bill Russell
9) Lenny Wilkens
10) Lenny Wilkens
11) Bob Pettit
12) George Gervin
13) Willis Reed
14) Bill Sharman
15) John Havlicek

40. All-Time Greats III

1) Kareem Abdul-Jabbar
2) Paul Arizin
3) Nate Archibald
4) Rick Barry
5) Kevin Porter
6) Wilt Chamberlain
7) Bob Cousy (1954)
8) Dave Cowens (1970–71)
9) Billy Cunningham
10) Dave DeBusschere
11) Bob Davies
12) Julius Erving
13) Joe Fulks
14) George Gervin
15) Walt Frazier

41. All-Time Greats IV

1) Hal Greer
2) John Havlicek
3) Sam Jones
4) Slater Martin
5) George Mikan
6) Earl Monroe
7) Bob Pettit
8) Willis Reed
9) Oscar Robertson
10) Bill Russell
11) Dolph Schayes
12) Bill Sharman
13) Jerry West
14) Lenny Wilkens
15) Elmore Smith

42. All-Time Greats V

1) Bill Sharman
2) Bill Russell (U. of San Francisco)
3) Oscar Robertson
4) George Mikan
5) Bob Cousy
6) Hal Greer
7) Joe Fulks
8) Dave DeBusschere
9) Bob Cousy
10) Paul Arizin
11) Jerry West (1964-65 Lakers)
12) Paul Arizin
13) Rick Barry
14) Dave DeBusschere
15) George Gervin (Squires)

43. All-Time Greats VI

1) Hal Greer
2) Slater Martin
3) George Mikan
4) Bob Pettit
5) John Havlicek
6) Bill Sharman
7) Lenny Wilkens (44)
8) George Yardley
9) Jerry West
10) Bill Sharman
11) Dolph Schayes
12) Bob Pettit
13) Slater Martin
14) Sam Jones
15) John Havlicek

44. All-Time Greats VII

1) Walt Frazier
2) Dave DeBusschere
3) Wilt Chamberlain
   (1966–67)
4) Paul Arizin
5) Jerry West
6) Nate Archibald
7) Rick Barry
8) Bob Cousy
9) Billy Cunningham
10) Wilt Chamberlain
11) George Gervin
12) Hal Greer
13) John Havlicek
14) Bob Pettit
15) Bill Russell

45. Rookie Years: Part I

1) Joe Fulks
2) Carl Braun
3) Dolph Schayes

46. Rookie Years: Part II

1) Ralph Beard
2) Bob Cousy
3) Neil Johnston
4) Jack McMahon
5) Clyde Lovellette
6) Larry Costello
7) Tom Gola
8) Bill Russell
9) Woody Sauldsberry
10) Elgin Baylor

47. Rookie Years: Part III

1) Wilt Chamberlain
2) Darrall Imhoff
3) Walt Bellamy
4) John Havlicek
5) Jerry Lucas
6) Happy Hairston
7) Rick Barry
8) Dave Bing
9) Bill Bradley
10) Elvin Hayes

48. Rookie Years: Part IV

1) Bob Dandridge
2) Nate Archibald
3) Julius Erving
4) George Gervin
5) Doug Collins
6) Moses Malone
7) Darryl Dawkins

8) Adrian Dantley
9) Bernard King
10) Mychal Thompson
11) Jim Paxson
12) Larry Smith
13) Kelly Tripucka

49. Career Countdown: Part I

1) Frank Baumholtz
2) Nat Hickey
3) Sid Tanenbaum
4) Ed Sadowski
5) Alex Groza
6) Cliff Barker
7) Fuzzy Levane

8) George Senesky
9) Bob Davies
10) George Mikan
11) Alex Hannum
12) Harry Gallatin
13) Vern Mikkelsen

50. Career Countdown: Part II

1) Dick McGuire
2) Bill Sharman
3) Paul Arizin
4) Dave Piontek
5) Frank Ramsey

6) Tom Heinsohn
7) John Kerr
8) K.C. Jones
9) Larry Costello
10) Wayne Embry

51. Career Countdown: Part III

1) Richie Guerin
2) Bailey Howell
3) Kevin Loughery
4) Hal Greer
5) Dave DeBusschere
6) Dave Stallworth

7) Billy Cunningham
8) Fred Carter
9) John Havlicek
10) Gail Goodrich
11) Dave Cowens
12) Jo Jo White

52. Sub-20-Point-a-Game Scorers

John Green
Bill Walton
Wes Unseld
Maurice Cheeks
Lucius Allen
Bob Davies
Tom Gola
Wayne Embry
Jim Pollard
Carl Braun
Jerry Sloan
Happy Hairston
Harry Gallatin

Dave DeBusschere
Vern Mikkelsen
Bill Bradley
Bill Russell
Guy Rodgers
Frank Ramsey
Larry Foust
John Kerr
Don Otten
Jon McGlocklin
Jim McMillian
Walter Dukes

53. 800 Assists

1) Nate Archibald
2) Kevin Porter
3) Michael Ray Richardson
4) Oscar Robertson
5) Guy Rodgers
6) Norm Van Lier

Flash Followup

1) Oscar Robertson

54. Good "D"

1) Yes
2) No
3) Yes
4) Yes
5) No
6) Yes
7) Yes
8) No
9) Yes
10) No
11) No
12) Yes
13) No
14) Yes
15) No
16) No

Flash Followup

1) Walt Frazier
2) Dave DeBusschere

55. Three-Point Shooters

Larry Bird (58)
Chris Ford (70)
Joe Hassett (69)
George McGinnis (62)
Brian Taylor (90)
Rick Barry (73)
John Brisker (89)
Roger Brown (63)
Glen Courtney Combs
  (130)
Louie Dampier (199)
Joe Hamilton (85)
Warren Jabali (102)

Stewart Johnson (64)
Bill Keller (123)
Wendell Ladner (61)
Dwight Lamar (69)
George Lehmann (154)
Fred Lewis (59)
Johnny Neumann (87)
Les Selvage (147)
Billy Shepherd (65)
George Stone (65)
Chico Vaughn (145)
Bob Verga (66)

56. Two-Team Champs

1) Royals and Celtics
2) Lakers and Hawks
3) Hawks and Celtics
4) 76ers and Lakers
5) Bucks and Bullets
6) Celtics and Sonics
7) Bucks and Lakers

57. Profile of a Champion

Philadelphia
1) Howie Dallmar
2) Art Hillhouse
3) George Senesky
4) Eddie Gottlieb

Baltimore
1) Connie Simmons
2) Kleggie Hermsen
3) Chick Reiser
4) Buddy Jeannette

Rochester
1) Arnie Johnson
2) Arnie Risen
3) Bobby Wanzer
4) Les Harrison

Minneapolis
1) Vern Mikkelsen
2) George Mikan
3) Bob Harrison
4) John Kundla

Syracuse
1) Earl Lloyd
2) John Kerr
3) Paul Seymour
4) Al Cervi

Philadelphia
1) Joe Graboski
2) Neil Johnston
3) Jack George
4) George Senesky

Boston
1) Jim Loscutoff
2) Bill Russell
3) Bill Sharman
4) Red Auerbach

St. Louis
1) Ed Macauley
2) Charlie Share
3) Jack McMahon
4) Alex Hannum

Philadelphia
1) Luke Jackson
2) Wilt Chamberlain
3) Larry Costello
4) Alex Hannum

Boston
1) Bailey Howell
2) Bill Russell
3) Sam Jones
4) Bill Russell

New York
1) Dave DeBusschere
2) Willis Reed
3) Dick Barnett
4) Red Holzman

Milwaukee
1) Greg Smith
2) Lew Alcindor
3) Oscar Robertson
4) Larry Costello

Los Angeles
1) Jim McMillian
2) Wilt Chamberlain
3) Gail Goodrich
4) Bill Sharman

Boston
1) Paul Silas
2) Dave Cowens
3) Jo Jo White
4) Tom Heinsohn

Golden State
1) Keith Wilkes
2) Clifford Ray
3) Butch Beard
4) Al Attles

Portland
1) Maurice Lucas
2) Bill Walton
3) Lionel Hollins
4) Jack Ramsay

Washington
1) Bob Dandridge
2) Wes Unseld
3) Phil Chenier
4) Dick Motta

Seattle
1) Lonnie Shelton
2) Jack Sikma
3) Dennis Johnson
4) Lennie Wilkens

Los Angeles
1) Jim Chones
2) Kareem Abdul-Jabbar
3) Norm Nixon
4) Jack McKinney-
   Paul Westhead

Boston
1) Cedric Maxwell
2) Robert Parish
3) Nate Archibald
4) Bill Fitch

58. Hall of Famers

Jerry West
Jerry Lucas
Paul Arizin
Joe Fulks
Dolph Schayes
Bill Sharman
Bob Pettit

Hal Greer
Elgin Baylor
Wilt Chamberlain
Bob Cousy
Cliff Hagan
Tom Gola
Frank Ramsey

Bob Davies   Andy Phillip
George Mikan   Bill Russell
Jim Pollard   Oscar Robertson
Ed Macauley

59. The Hall of Fame

1) Paul Arizin   17) Ed Macauley
2) Red Auerbach   18) George Mikan
3) Elgin Baylor   19) Bob Pettit
4) Walter Brown   20) Andy Phillip
5) Wilt Chamberlain   21) Maurice Podoloff
6) Bob Cousy   22) Jim Pollard
7) Bob Davies   23) Oscar Robertson
8) Joe Fulks   24) Bill Russell
9) Tom Gola   25) Dolph Schayes
10) Eddie Gottlieb   26) Bill Sharman
11) Cliff Hagan   27) Jerry West
12) Les Harrison   28) Frank Ramsey
13) Ned Irish   29) Slater Martin
14) Pat Kennedy   30) Willis Reed
15) Walter Kennedy   31) Hal Greer
16) Jerry Lucas

60. Full-Court Press

1) Kevin Porter   12) Bill Sharman
2) Elmore Smith   13) Bill Walton
3) Randy Smith   14) Jerry West
4) Brian Taylor   15) Walt Frazier
5) David Thompson   16) Joe Fulks
6) Neil Johnston   17) Hal Greer
7) Sam Jones   18) John Havlicek
8) Jerry Lucas   19) Kareem Abdul-Jabbar
9) Willis Reed   20) Mack Calvin
10) Oscar Robertson   21) Julius Erving
11) Bill Russell   22) George Gervin

23) Artis Gilmore   27) Cedric Maxwell
24) Dan Issel   28) Swen Nater
25) Caldwell Jones   29) David Thompson
26) Bobby Jones   30) Bill Russell

61. Name That Team

1) Warriors   9) Rockets   17) Bullets
2) Lakers   10) Kings   18) Hawks
3) Suns   11) Spurs   19) Bulls
4) Trail Blazers 12) Jazz   20) Cavaliers
5) Clippers   13) Celtics   21) Pistons
6) SuperSonics 14) Nets   22) Pacers
7) Mavericks   15) Knicks   23) Bucks
8) Nuggets   16) 76ers

62. Conference and Division Play

Eastern Conference

Atlantic Division   ### Central Division
1) Philadelphia   6) Milwaukee
2) Boston   7) Indiana
3) New Jersey   8) Atlanta
4) Washington   9) Detroit
5) New York   10) Chicago
                                 11) Cleveland

Western Conference

Midwest Division   ### Pacific Division
12) San Antonio   18) Los Angeles
13) Houston   19) Seattle
14) Denver   20) Golden State
15) Utah   21) Phoenix
16) Dallas   22) Portland
17) Kansas City   23) San Diego

63. Championship Clubs

1) Philadelphia		19) Boston	
2) Baltimore		20) Boston	
3) Minneapolis		21) Philadelphia	
4) Minneapolis		22) Boston	
5) Rochester		23) Boston	
6) Minneapolis		24) New York	
7) Minneapolis		25) Milwaukee	
8) Minneapolis		26) Los Angeles	
9) Syracuse		27) New York	
10) Philadelphia		28) Boston	
11) Boston		29) Golden State	
12) St. Louis		30) Boston	
13) Boston		31) Portland	
14) Boston		32) Washington	
15) Boston		33) Seattle	
16) Boston		34) Los Angeles	
17) Boston		35) Boston	
18) Boston		36) Los Angeles	

64. Once Upon a Time

1) e	5) m	9) l	13) b
2) i	6) g	10) f	14) o
3) d	7) n	11) h	15) j
4) k	8) a	12) p	16) c

65. Setting the Record Straight

1) C	7) I	13) C	19) I
2) C	8) C	14) I	20) C
3) I	9) C	15) C	21) C
4) I	10) I	16) I	22) C
5) I	11) C	17) C	23) I
6) C	12) I	18) C	24) I

25) I	39) I	53) C	67) I
26) C	40) C	54) C	68) I
27) C	41) C	55) I	69) I
28) I	42) C	56) I	70) I
29) C	43) I	57) C	71) I
30) C	44) C	58) C	72) C
31) C	45) I	59) I	73) C
32) C	46) C	60) C	74) I
33) I	47) I	61) I	75) I
34) C	48) I	62) C	76) C
35) I	49) I	63) I	77) C
36) C	50) C	64) I	78) I
37) C	51) C	65) C	
38) C	52) C	66) C	

66. Record (Team) Review

1) Lakers (1971–72)
2) 76ers (1972–73)
3) Lakers (1976–77 and 1979–80)
4) Rockets (1967–68)
5) Celtics (1972–73 and 1974–75)
6) Pistons (1979–80)
7) Olympians (1951)
8) Royals
9) Lakers (1971–72)
10) Capitols (1948)
11) 76ers (1966–67)
12) 76ers (1973)
13) Lakers (1970)
14) 76ers (1966–67)
15) Sonics (1967–68)
16) Lakers (1979–80)
17) Kings (1974–75)
18) Celtics (1960–61)
19) Bucks (1978–79)
20) Lakers (1971–72)
21) Nationals (1960–61)
22) Celtics (1959)
23) 76ers (1966)

67. Pro Debuts

1) Seattle (1969–70)
2) Syracuse (1959–60)
3) Philadelphia (1954–55)
4) Detroit (1962–63)
5) Ft. Wayne (1950–51)
6) Los Angeles (1965–66)
7) Syracuse (1958–59)

8) Phoenix (1969–70)	17) Milwaukee (1954–55)
9) Denver (1969–70)	18) Chicago (1947–48)
10) New York (1964–65)	19) Indianapolis (1945–46)
11) Minneapolis (1959–60)	20) New York (1966–67)
12) Detroit (1962–63)	21) Washington (1950–51)
13) Cincinnati (1966–67)	22) Philadelphia (1954–55)
14) St. Louis (1949–50)	23) St. Louis (1964–65)
15) Atlanta (1970–71)	24) Baltimore (1965–66)
16) Chicago (1946–47)	25) Syracuse (1962–63)

68. Breaking In

1) Cincinnati (1970–71)	14) Detroit (1970–71)
2) Philadelphia (1970–71)	15) Utah (1974–75)
3) New York (1972–73)	16) Detroit (1969–70)
4) Philadelphia (1974–75)	17) San Diego (1970–71)
5) Buffalo (1976–77)	18) Baltimore (1972–73)
6) Milwaukee (1976–77)	19) San Antonio (1976–77)
7) Philadelphia (1975–76)	20) Phoenix (1975–76)
8) San Antonio (1976–77)	21) Kansas City (1976–77)
9) San Diego (1968–69)	22) Cleveland (1974–75)
10) Portland (1975–76)	23) Denver (1976–77)
11) Chicago (1974–75)	24) Boston (1972–73)
12) Atlanta (1973–74)	25) Portland (1971–72)
13) New York (1973–74)	

69. Bowing Out

1) Houston (1979–80)	8) Atlanta (1969–70)
2) Los Angeles (1974–75)	9) St. Louis (1965–66)
3) Boston (1977–78)	10) Philadelphia (1970–71)
4) Milwaukee (1976–77)	11) Baltimore (1965–66)
5) Cincinnati (1969)	12) San Francisco (1968–69)
6) St. Louis (1961–62)	
7) New Orleans (1978–79)	13) Boston (1963–64)

14) St. Louis (1959–60)	20) Boston (1957–58)
15) Detroit (1959–60)	21) Milwaukee (1969–70)
16) Baltimore (1954–55)	22) Chicago (1977–78)
17) Seattle (1970–71)	23) Cleveland (1976–77)
18) Boston (1965–66)	24) Kansas City (1980–81)
19) Atlanta (1969–70)	25) Ft. Wayne (1955–56)

70. The Trailblazers

Celtics

1) Pete Barry	5) Joe Lapchick
2) Dutch Dehnert	6) Davey Banks
3) Nat Holman	7) Ernie Reich
4) Johnny Beckman	

Rens

1) Clarence Jenkins	5) Eyre Saitch
2) Bill Yancey	6) Willie Smith
3) Casey Holt	7) Tarzan Cooper
4) Pappy Ricks	

Germans

1) Al Heerdt
2) William Rhode
3) George Redlein
4) Alfred Manweiler
5) Ed Miller
6) Hank Faust
7) Ed Reimann

71. High-Percentage Winners

1) Philadelphia (.840 in 1966–67)
2) Milwaukee (.805 in 1970–71)
3) Los Angeles (.841 in 1971–72)
4) Boston (.829 in 1971–72)

72. High-Percentage Second-Place Finishers

1) Philadelphia (.720 in 1979–80
   and .756 in 1980–81)
2) Minneapolis (.750 in 1948–49)
3) Rochester (.750 in 1949–50)
4) Boston (.741 in 1966–67)

73. Low-Percentage Winners

1) St. Louis (.472 in 1956–57)
2) Baltimore (.463 in 1971–72)
3) Milwaukee (.463 in 1975–76)

74. Team Magnates

1) f	6) d
2) j	7) c
3) a	8) i
4) h	9) e
5) b	10) g

75. Team Colors

1) Royal Purple and Gold
2) Red, White, and Blue
3) Green and White
4) Red, White, and Blue
5) Red, White, and Blue
6) Red, White, and Gold
7) Blue and Green
8) Red, White, and Blue
9) Red, White, and Black
10) Forest Green, Red, and White
11) Green and Gold
12) Red, White, and Blue
13) Scarlet, Black, and White
14) Purple, Green, and Gold
15) Metallic Silver and Black
16) Wine and Gold
17) Purple, Orange, and Copper
18) Red, White, and Blue
19) Red and Gold
20) Blue and Gold

76. Retired Numbers

1) Bob Pettit
2) Lou Hudson
1) Walter Brown
2) Bill Russell
3) Jo Jo White
4) Bob Cousy
5) Tom Heinsohn
6) Tom Sanders
7) John Havlicek
8) Dave Cowens
9) Don Nelson
10) Bill Sharman
11) Ed Macauley
12) Frank Ramsey
13) Sam Jones
14) K.C. Jones
1) Jerry Sloan
1) Bingo Smith
2) Austin Carr
3) Nate Thurmond
1) Byron Beck
1) Tom Meschery
2) Al Attles

3) Nate Thurmond
1) Maurice Stokes
2) Oscar Robertson
3) Jack Twyman
1) Elgin Baylor
1) Oscar Robertson
2) Jon McGlocklin
1) Wendell Ladner
2) Bill Melchionni
1) Walt Frazier
2) Willis Reed
3) Dave DeBusschere
1) Hal Greer
2) Billy Cunningham
1) Dick Van Arsdale
2) Connie Hawkins
1) Dave Twardzik
2) Larry Steele
3) Lloyd Neal
4) Geoff Petrie
1) Lenny Wilkens
1) Wes Unseld

THE THIRD QUARTER

77. Scoring Champions

1) Joe Fulks
2) Paul Arizin
3) Neil Johnston
4) Wilt Chamberlain
5) George Yardley
6) Dave Bing
7) Wilt Chamberlain
8) Rick Barry
9) Max Zaslofsky
10) George Mikan
11) Bob Pettit
12) Elvin Hayes
13) Jerry West
14) Bob McAdoo
15) Nate Archibald
16) Pete Maravich
17) George Gervin
18) Adrian Dantley

78. Once Is Not Enough

1) Wilt Chamberlain
2) Neil Johnston
3) George Mikan
4) Bob McAdoo
5) George Gervin
6) Paul Arizin
7) Bob Pettit
8) Kareem Abdul-Jabbar

79. They Made Their Point

1) Wilt Chamberlain
2) Kareem Abdul-Jabbar
3) Oscar Robertson
4) John Havlicek
5) Jerry West
6) Elvin Hayes
7) Elgin Baylor
8) Hal Greer
9) Walt Bellamy

Flash Followup

1) Wilt Chamberlain

80. Super Scorers

1) Wilt Chamberlain
2) David Thompson
3) Elgin Baylor
4) Pete Maravich
5) Rick Barry
6) Joe Fulks
7) Jerry West
8) George Gervin
9) George Mikan

Flash Followup

1) Wilt Chamberlain

81. Field Goal Marksmen

1) Artis Gilmore (.577)
2) Kareem Abdul-Jabbar (.556)
3) Bobby Jones (.552)
4) Walter Davis (.547)
5) Marques Johnson (.542)
6) Adrian Dantley (.540)
7) Swen Nater (.539)
8) George Gervin (.527)
9) Bernard King (.524)

Flash Followup

1) Wilt Chamberlain (.540)

82. The Boardmen

1) Wilt Chamberlain
2) Bill Russell
3) Elvin Hayes
4) Nate Thurmond
5) Walt Bellamy
6) Wes Unseld
7) Kareem Abdul-Jabbar
8) Jerry Lucas
9) Bob Pettit

Flash Followup

1) Wilt Chamberlain

83. They Couldn't Resist the Assist

1) Oscar Robertson
2) Lenny Wilkens
3) Bob Cousy
4) Guy Rodgers
5) Jerry West
6) John Havlicek
7) Dave Bing
8) Nate Archibald
9) Kevin Porter

Flash Followup

1) Oscar Robertson

84. .900-Plus Free-Throw Shooters

1) Calvin Murphy
2) Rick Barry
3) Ernie Di Gregorio
4) Ricky Sobers
5) Bill Sharman
6) Bobby Wanzer
7) Dolph Schayes
8) Adrian Smith

85. They Were Fine on the Line

1) Oscar Robertson
2) Jerry West
3) Dolph Schayes
4) Bob Pettit
5) Wilt Chamberlain
6) Elgin Baylor
7) Lenny Wilkens
8) John Havlicek
9) Walt Bellamy

Flash Followup

1) Oscar Robertson

86. Free Throw Marksmen

1) Rick Barry
2) Calvin Murphy
3) Bill Sharman
4) Mike Newlin
5) Fred Brown
6) Ricky Sobers
7) Larry Siegfried
8) Flynn Robinson
9) Brian Winters

Flash Followup

1) Rick Barry

87. 43-Minute Games

1) Kareem Abdul-Jabbar
2) Nate Archibald
3) Julius Erving
4) Artis Gilmore
5) Elvin Hayes
6) Dan Issel
7) Bob McAdoo
8) Truck Robinson

Flash Followup

1) Artis Gilmore
2) Elvin Hayes

88. Most Minutes

1) Wilt Chamberlain
2) John Havlicek
3) Elvin Hayes
4) Oscar Robertson
5) Bill Russell

Flash Followup

1) Wilt Chamberlain

89. Fair or Foul

1) Vern Mikkelsen
2) Walter Dukes
3) Charlie Share
4) Paul Arizin
5) Tom Gola

6) Tom Sanders
7) Bailey Howell
8) Dolph Schayes
9) Tom Meschery

Flash Followup

1) Vern Mikkelsen

90. Nothing Personal

1) Hal Greer
2) Dolph Schayes
3) Elvin Hayes
4) Walt Bellamy
5) Bailey Howell

6) Bill Bridges
7) Lenny Wilkens
8) John Havlicek
9) Sam Lacey

Flash Followup

1) Hal Greer

91. Most Games

1) John Havlicek
2) Paul Silas
3) Hal Greer
4) Lenny Wilkens
5) Elvin Hayes

6) Dolph Schayes
7) Johnny Green
8) Don Nelson
9) Leroy Ellis

Flash Followup

1) John Havlicek

92. MVP Awards

1) Bob Cousy
2) Bill Russell
3) Dave Cowens
4) Wilt Chamberlain
5) Julius Erving
6) Bob Pettit
7) Oscar Robertson
8) Wes Unseld
9) Willis Reed
10) Kareem Abdul-Jabbar
11) Bob McAdoo
12) Bill Walton
13) Moses Malone
14) Kareem Abdul-Jabbar

93. Once Is Not Enough: II

1) Kareem Abdul-Jabbar
2) Bill Russell
3) Wilt Chamberlain
4) Bob Pettit

94. Shooting Highs

1) Wilt Chamberlain
2) Elgin Baylor
3) Paul Westphal
4) Geoff Petrie
5) Bob McAdoo
6) Fred Brown
7) Abdul Jeelani
8) David Thompson
9) Calvin Murphy
10) Jack Twyman
11) George Gervin
12) Pete Maravich
13) Sam Jones
14) Julius Erving
15) Richie Guerin
16) Wilt Chamberlain
17) Earl Monroe
18) Bob Pettit and
    Lou Hudson
19) Kareem Abdul-Jabbar
20) Chet Walker
21) Walt Wesley
22) Dave Bing
23) George McGinnis

95. The Assistmen

1) Guy Rodgers
2) Jerry West
3) Gail Goodrich
4) Rick Adelman
5) Ernie Di Gregorio
6) Lenny Wilkens
7) Brad Davis
8) Larry Brown
9) Art Williams
10) Oscar Robertson and Phil Ford
11) Johnny Moore
12) Gail Goodrich
13) Bob Cousy
14) Kevin Porter
15) Richie Guerin
16) Wilt Chamberlain
17) Kevin Porter
18) Walt Hazzard and Lenny Wilkens
19) Clem Haskins
20) Lenny Wilkens and Bobby Washington
21) Kevin Porter
22) Don Buse
23) Guy Rodgers

96. The Boardmen

1) Wilt Chamberlain
2) Wilt Chamberlain
3) Paul Silas
4) Sidney Wicks
5) Swen Nater
6) Jim Fox
7) Bill Robinzine
8) Spencer Haywood
9) Elvin Hayes
10) Jerry Lucas
11) Manny Leaks
12) Len Robinson
13) Bill Russell
14) Billy Paultz
15) Harry Gallatin
16) Wilt Chamberlain
17) Walt Bellamy
18) Bob Pettit
19) Tom Boerwinkle
20) Rick Roberson
21) Bob Lanier
22) George McGinnis
23) Swen Nater

97. Club's All-Time Point Leaders

1) Bob Pettit
2) John Havlicek
3) Bob Love
4) Austin Carr
5) Jim Spanarkel
6) David Thompson
7) Bob Lanier
8) Wilt Chamberlain

9) Calvin Murphy
10) Roger Brown
11) Oscar Robertson
12) Jerry West
13) Kareem Abdul-Jabbar
14) John Williamson
15) Walt Frazier
16) Hal Greer

17) Dick Van Arsdale
18) Geoff Petrie
19) George Gervin
20) Randy Smith
21) Fred Brown
22) Pete Maravich
23) Elvin Hayes

98. Club's All-Time Assist Leaders

1) Lenny Wilkens
2) Bob Cousy
3) Norm Van Lier
4) Foots Walker
5) Brad Davis
6) Ralph Simpson
7) Dave Bing
8) Guy Rodgers
9) Calvin Murphy
10) Freddie Lewis
11) Oscar Robertson
12) Jerry West

13) Oscar Robertson
14) Bill Melchionni
15) Walt Frazier
16) Hal Greer
17) Dick Van Arsdale
18) Geoff Petrie
19) James Silas
20) Randy Smith
21) Lenny Wilkens
22) Pete Maravich
23) Wes Unseld

99. Club's All-Time Rebound Leaders

1) Bob Pettit
2) Bill Russell
3) Tom Boerwinkle
4) Jim Chones
5) Tom Lagarde
6) Byron Beck
7) Bob Lanier
8) Nate Thurmond
9) Rudy Tomjanovich
10) Mel Daniels
11) Jerry Lucas
12) Elgin Baylor

13) Kareem Abdul-Jabbar
14) Billy Paultz
15) Willis Reed
16) Dolph Schayes
17) Neal Walk
18) Sidney Wicks
19) Larry Kenon
20) Bob McAdoo
21) Spencer Haywood
22) Len Robinson
23) Wes Unseld

100. NBA Game Records

1) Wilt Chamberlain
2) Wilt Chamberlain
3) Bob Pettit
4) Wilt Chamberlain
5) Kevin Porter
6) Don Otten

101. NBA Season Records

1) Wilt Chamberlain
2) Wilt Chamberlain
3) Brian Taylor
4) Wilt Chamberlain
5) Fred Brown
6) Jerry West
7) Calvin Murphy
8) Wilt Chamberlain
9) Kevin Porter
10) Bill Robinzine

102. Playoff: Preliminary Series

1) Wilt Chamberlain
2) Bob Cousy
3) Bob Cousy
4) Wilt Chamberlain
5) Wilt Chamberlain
6) Jerry West
7) Norm Nixon

103. Championship Series

1) Elgin Baylor
2) Rick Barry
3) Bob Pettit
4) Bill Russell
5) Bob Cousy
6) Walt Frazier

104. ABA Single-Game Records

1) c
2) e
3) f
4) a
5) d
6) b

105. ABA Season Records

1) b
2) d
3) g
4) a
5) h

6) f
7) i
8) e
9) c

106. ABA Career Records

1) Louie Dampier
2) Julius Erving
3) Mel Daniels (4,692)
4) Louie Dampier
5) Mack Calvin
6) Mel Daniels

7) Louie Dampier
8) Louie Dampier
9) Jim Logan
10) Gene Moore
11) Louie Dampier

107. Multiple ABA First-Team Selections

Connie Hawkins
Mel Daniels
Larry Jones
Rick Barry
James Jones

Mack Calvin
Artis Gilmore
Julius Erving
George McGinnis

108. ABA's Who's Who

1) Artis Gilmore
2) Mel Daniels
3) Rick Barry
4) Julius Erving
5) Connie Hawkins
6) Mel Daniels
7) Mel Daniels

8) Spencer Haywood (1970)
9) Artis Gilmore (1972)
10) Julius Erving (He tied one of the three times.)
11) Mel Daniels (twice)

109. A Matter of Association

1) NBA	18) NBA	35) NBA
2) NBA	19) NBA	36) NAN
3) NAN	20) NBA	37) NBA
4) ABA	21) ABA	38) NBA
5) NBA	22) NAN	39) ABA
6) ABA	23) ABA	40) NAN
7) ABA	24) ABA	41) NBA
8) NAN	25) ABA	42) ABA
9) ABA	26) NAN	43) NBA
10) NBA	27) NBA	44) NBA
11) NBA	28) ABA	45) ABA
12) NBA	29) NBA	46) NBA
13) ABA	30) NBA	47) NAN
14) NAN	31) NAN	48) NBA
15) ABA	32) NBA	49) NBA
16) ABA	33) ABA	
17) NAN	34) NBA	

110. Two-Dimensional Players

1) Mel Daniels
2) Dick Barnett
3) Wilt Chamberlain
4) Julius Erving
5) Connie Hawkins
6) Billy Cunningham
7) Dan Issel or Artis Gilmore
8) Spencer Haywood
9) Rick Barry
10) Artis Gilmore or Dan Issel

111. Super (ABA) Scorers

1) Rick Barry
2) Connie Hawkins
3) Spencer Haywood
4) Charlie Scott
5) Dan Issel
6) Julius Erving

Flash Followup

1) Rick Barry

112. First-Team All Stars

Joe Fulks (3-2)
Max Zaslofsky (4-3)
Jim Pollard (2-1)
Alex Groza (2-1)
Spencer Haywood (2-1)
Bob Davies (4-3)
Dave Bing (2-1)
Bill Sharman (4-3)
George Mikan (6-5)

Bob Cousy (10-9)
Elgin Baylor (10-9)
Pete Maravich (2-1)
Neil Johnston (4-3)
Bob Pettit (10-6)
Jerry West (10-7)
Walt Frazier (4-3)
John Havlicek (4-3)

Flash Followup

1) Bob Cousy
2) Bob Pettit

3) Elgin Baylor
4) Jerry West

113. Once A Bridesmaid . . .

First Team
1) Howie Dallmar
2) Harry Gallatin
3) Larry Foust
4) Gene Shue
5) Wes Unseld
6) Earl Monroe
7) Connie Hawkins
8) Willis Reed
9) Gail Goodrich
10) Bob McAdoo
11) George McGinnis

Second Team
1) John Logan
2) Vern Mikkelsen
3) Bobby Wanzer
4) Slater Martin
5) Maurice Stokes
6) Richie Guerin
7) Tommy Heinsohn
8) Hal Greer
9) Sam Jones
10) Dave Cowens
11) Gus Johnson

Flash Followup

1) Hal Greer
2) Vern Mikkelsen (4)
3) Tommy Heinsohn (4)

4) Gus Johnson (4)
5) Slater Martin (5)

114. All-Star MVPs

1) a	12) c	23) b
2) b	13) c	24) c
3) b	14) c	25) c
4) a	15) a	26) a
5) c	16) c	27) a
6) a	17) b	28) c
7) a	18) a	29) b
8) c	19) b	30) b
9) a and c	20) a	31) b
10) b	21) b	32) a
11) a	22) c	

115. Double-Digit Assistmen

1) Dick McGuire
2) Bob Cousy
3) Oscar Robertson
4) Guy Rodgers

Flash Followup

1) Oscar Robertson
2) Mack Calvin (11)
2) Mack Calvin (11), Freddie Lewis (10)

116. The Bounders

1) Bob Pettit
2) Wilt Chamberlain
3) Bill Russell
4) Dave Cowens

Flash Followup

1) Bob Pettit
2) Swen Nater (22)

117. 30-Point Shooters

1) Elgin Baylor
2) Wilt Chamberlain
3) Rick Barry
4) Walt Frazier

5) Julius Erving
6) Bob McAdoo
7) George Gervin

Flash Followup

1) Wilt Chamberlain

2) Larry Jones (30)

118. All-Star Matchups

1) John Havlicek
2) Wilt Chamberlain
3) Bob Pettit
4) Oscar Robertson
5) Oscar Robertson
6) Elgin Baylor
7) Archie Clark
8) Oscar Robertson

9) Wilt Chamberlain
10) Bob Pettit
11) Bob Cousy
12) Dolph Schayes
13) Randy Smith
14) Jerry West
15) Rick Barry

THE FOURTH QUARTER

119. Career Points

Below 10,000

1) Bill Bradley (9,217)
2) Fred Carter (9,271)
3) Larry Costello (8,622)
4) Bob Davies (7,770)
5) Connie Dierking (7,094)
6) Terry Dischinger (9,012)
7) Ray Felix (6,974)
8) Joe Fulks (8,003)
9) Harry Gallatin (8,843)
10) Tom Gola (7,871)
11) Butch Komives (7,550)
12) Slater Martin (7,337)
13) Jon McGlocklin (9,169)
14) Dick McGuire (5,921)
15) Jim McMillian (8,736)
16) Andy Phillip (6,384)
17) Jim Pollard (6,522)
18) Frank Ramsey (8,378)
19) George Yardley (9,063)

Between 10,000 and 15,000

1) Dave Cowens (13,092)
2) Dave DeBusschere (14,053)
3) Wayne Embry (10,380)
4) Richie Guerin (14,676)
5) Cliff Hagan (14,870)
6) Happy Hairston (11,505)
7) Tom Heinsohn (12,194)
8) Neil Johnston (10,023)
9) John Kerr (12,480)
10) Kevin Loughery (11,130)
11) Bob Love (13,895)
12) Clyde Lovellette (11,947)
13) Ed Macauley (11,234)
14) Jack Marin (12,541)
15) George Mikan (11,764)
16) Don Nelson (10,898)
17) Willis Reed (12,183)
18) Bill Russell (14,522)

19) Bill Sharman (12,665)

20) Nate Thurmond (14,437)

Between 15,000 and 20,000

1) Paul Arizin (16,266)
2) Dick Barnett (15,358)
3) Zelmo Beatty (15,205)
4) Bob Cousy (16,960)
5) Billy Cunningham (16,310)
6) Walt Frazier (15,581)
7) Gail Goodrich (19,181)
8) Spencer Haywood (15,789)
9) Bailey Howell (17,770)
10) Lou Hudson (17,940)
11) Sam Jones (15,380)
12) Pete Maravich (15,948)
13) Earl Monroe (17,454)
14) Dolph Schayes (19,247)
15) Jack Twyman (15,840)
16) Chet Walker (18,831)
17) Len Wilkens (17,772)

Above 20,000

1) Rick Barry (25,279)
2) Elgin Baylor (23,149)
3) Walt Bellamy (20,941)
4) Hal Greer (21,586)
5) John Havlicek (26,395)
6) Bob Pettit (20,880)
7) Oscar Robertson (26,710)
8) Jerry West (25,192)

120. Career Averages

Eight to 12 Points

1) Connie Dierking (10.0)
2) Ray Felix (10.9)
3) Tom Gola (11.3)
4) Butch Komives (10.2)
5) Slater Martin (9.8)
6) Jon McGlocklin (11.6)
7) Dick McGuire (8.0)
8) Don Nelson (10.3)
9) Andy Phillip (9.1)

12 to 16 Points

1) Dick Barnett (15.8)
2) Bill Bradley (12.4)
3) Fred Carter (15.2)
4) Larry Costello (12.2)
5) Bob Davies (13.7)
6) Terry Dischinger (13.8)
7) Wayne Embry (12.5)
8) Harry Gallatin (13.0)
9) Happy Hairston (14.8)
10) John Kerr (13.8)
11) Kevin Loughery (15.4)
12) Jack Marin (14.8)
13) Jim McMillian (13.8)
14) Jim Pollard (13.1)
15) Frank Ramsey (13.4)
16) Bill Russell (15.1)
17) Nate Thurmond (15.0)

16 to 20 Points

1) Zelmo Beatty (17.1)
2) Bob Cousy (18.4)
3) Dave Cowens (18.0)
4) Dave DeBusschere (16.1)
5) Walt Frazier (18.9)
6) Joe Fulks (16.4)
7) Gail Goodrich (18.6)
8) Hal Greer (19.2)
9) Cliff Hagan (17.7)
10) Tom Heinsohn (18.6)
11) Bailey Howell (18.7)
12) Neil Johnston (19.4)
13) Sam Jones (17.6)
14) Bob Love (17.6)
15) Clyde Lovellette (17.0)
16) Ed Macauley (17.5)
17) Earl Monroe (18.8)
18) Willis Reed (18.7)
19) Dolph Schayes (18.2)
20) Bill Sharman (17.8)
21) Jack Twyman (19.2)
22) Chet Walker (18.2)
23) Len Wilkens (16.5)
24) George Yardley (19.2)
25) Richie Guerin (17.3)

20 to 24 Points

1) Paul Arizin (22.8)
2) Walt Bellamy (20.1)
3) Billy Cunningham (21.2)
4) John Havlicek (20.8)
5) Spencer Haywood (21.6)
6) Lou Hudson (20.2)
7) George Mikan (22.6)

24 or More Points

1) Rick Barry (24.8)
2) Elgin Baylor (27.4)

3) Pete Maravich (24.2)   5) Oscar Robertson (25.7)
4) Bob Pettit (26.4)   6) Jerry West (27.0)

121. 30-Point Seasons

1) Nate Archibald   6) Spencer Haywood
2) Julius Erving   7) Pete Maravich
3) Dan Issel   8) Bob Pettit
4) Walt Bellamy   9) Jack Twyman
5) Connie Hawkins

122. Multiple 30-Point Seasons

1) Wilt Chamberlain   5) Kareem Abdul-Jabbar
2) Oscar Robertson   6) Elgin Baylor
3) Jerry West   7) Bob McAdoo
4) Rick Barry

123. Good Is Just Not Good Enough

1) Rick Barry (753)   6) Lloyd Free (654)
2) Elgin Baylor (676)   7) Bob Pettit (695)
3) Wilt Chamberlain   8) Oscar Robertson
   (835)   (800)
4) Nate Archibald (677)   9) Dolph Schayes (680)
5) Mack Calvin (696)   10) Jerry West (840)

Flash Followup

1) Oscar Robertson   4) Bob Pettit (6,182)
   (7,694)   5) Wilt Chamberlain
2) Jerry West (7,160)   (6,057)
3) Dolph Schayes (6,979)

124. The Right Height

7-0 to 7-3

1) Henry Finkel (7-0)
2) Wilt Chamberlain (7-1)
3) Mel Counts (7-0)
4) Ron Taylor (7-1)
5) Walter Dukes (7-0)
6) Dave Newmark (7-0)
7) Luke Witte (7-0)
8) Greg Fillmore (7-1)
9) Swede Halbrook (7-3)
10) Jim McDaniels (7-0)

6-8 to 6-11

1) Bill Walton (6-11)
2) Marvin Barnes (6-9)
3) John Kerr (6-9)
4) Len Chappell (6-8)
5) Connie Dierking (6-10)
6) Mel Daniels (6-9)
7) Leroy Ellis (6-10)
8) Larry Foust (6-9)
9) Nate Thurmond (6-11)
10) Dolph Schayes (6-8)

6-4 to 6-7

1) Paul Arizin (6-4)
2) Chet Walker (6-6)
3) Alex Groza (6-7)
4) Don Chaney (6-5)
5) Rick Barry (6-7)
6) Larry Siegfried (6-4)
7) Elgin Baylor (6-5)
8) Vince Boryla (6-5)
9) Ed Conlin (6-6)
10) Howie Dallmar (6-4)

6-0 to 6-3

1) Guy Rodgers (6-0)
2) Lucius Allen (6-2)
3) Andy Phillip (6-2)
4) Johnny Egan (6-0)
5) Frank Brian (6-1)
6) Al Bianchi (6-3)
7) Fred Carter (6-3)
8) Sihugo Green (6-2)
9) Archie Clark (6-2)
10) Bob Davies (6-1)

5-8 to 5-11

1) Ralph Beard (5-10)
2) Fred Scolari (5-10)
3) Joe Hamilton (5-10)
4) Kenny Sailors (5-10)
5) Ernie Calverley (5-10)

6) Al Cervi (5-11)
7) Mel Riebe (5-11)
8) Chick Reiser (5-11)

9) Sonny Hertzberg (5-10)
10) Slater Martin (5-10)

125. Matching Nicknames

1) Jim Barnes
2) Zelmo Beaty
3) Walt Bellamy
4) Robert Boozer
5) Harry Boykoff
6) Joe Caldwell
7) Don Carlson
8) Al Cervi
9) Don Chaney
10) Nat Clifton
11) Kevin Connors
12) Wayne Embry
13) Walt Frazier
14) Joe Fulks
15) Harry Gallatin
16) George Glamack
17) Joe Graboski
18) Harry Grant
19) Harold Hairston
20) John Havlicek
21) Sidney Hertzberg
22) Paul Hoffman
23) William Holzman
24) Rodney Hundley
25) Leslie Hunter
26) Wallace Jones
27) James King
28) Robert Kinney
29) Leo Klier
30) Howard Komives
31) David Lattin
32) Robert Leonard

33) Andrew Levane
34) Earl Lloyd
35) James Loscutoff
36) Kevin Loughery
37) Ed Macauley
38) Slater Martin
39) Bill McGill
40) Richard McGuire
41) Horace McKinney
42) Don Meineke
43) Earl Monroe
44) Jeff Mullins
45) Charles Nash
46) Joseph Reiser
47) Arnold Risen
48) Oscar Robertson
49) Ephraim Rocha
50) Tom Sanders
51) Frank Saul
52) Howard Schultz
53) Ken Sears
54) Jerry Sloan
55) Adrian Smith
56) Bobby Smith
57) Arthur Spector
58) Dave Stallworth
59) Harley Swift
60) William Van Breda Kolff
61) Bob Warren
62) Tom Washington
63) Don Watts

64) Joseph White
65) Art Williams
66) Max Zaslofsky
67) Robert Zawoluk
68) Paul Arizin

69) Jerry West
70) Wilt Chamberlain
71) Billy Cunningham
72) Bob Davies

126. Old NBA Numbers

1) Oscar Robertson
   (Bucks)
2) Dolph Schayes
3) Neil Johnston
4) Bill Russell
5) Pete Maravich
6) Bob Pettit
7) Joe Fulks
8) Walt Frazier
9) Bob Davies
10) Paul Arizin
11) George Yardley
12) Dick Barnett
13) Wilt Chamberlain
14) Bob Cousy
15) Tom Gola
16) Earl Monroe
17) Red Holzman
18) Cliff Hagan
19) Jerry Lucas
20) John Havlicek
21) Dave Cowens
22) Nat Clifton

23) Lenny Wilkens
24) Willis Reed
25) Ed Macauley (Hawks)
26) Bill Sharman
27) Slater Martin
28) Elgin Baylor
29) Dave DeBusschere
30) Frank Ramsey
31) Spencer Haywood
32) Rick Barry
33) K.C. Jones
34) Chet Walker
35) Jack Twyman
36) Wayne Embry
37) Billy Cunningham
38) Cazzie Russell
39) Clyde Lovellette
40) Paul Silas
41) Wes Unseld
42) Jerry West
43) Phil Chenier
44) George Mikan

127. Player Positions

1) Guard
2) Forward
3) Center

4) Guard
5) Guard
6) Center

7) Forward	24) Guard
8) Forward	25) Guard
9) Guard	26) Center
10) Forward	27) Forward
11) Center	28) Center
12) Center	29) Forward
13) Guard	30) Guard
14) Forward	31) Guard
15) Forward	32) Guard
16) Guard	33) Forward
17) Forward	34) Guard
18) Guard	35) Forward
19) Center	36) Forward
20) Forward	37) Forward
21) Center	38) Guard
22) Forward	39) Center
23) Center	40) Center

128. College Ball

1) i	8) p	15) q	22) t
2) r	9) l	16) m	23) j
3) a	10) b	17) w	24) v
4) n	11) y	18) k	25) g
5) x	12) f	19) o	
6) u	13) s	20) h	
7) c	14) d	21) e	

129. One-Team Players

1) Paul Arizin
   (Warriors, 10)
2) Al Attles
   (Warriors, 11)
3) Elgin Baylor
   (Lakers, 14)
4) Al Bianchi
   (Nats-Warriors, 10)
5) Tom Boerwinkle
   (Bulls, 10)
6) Bill Bradley
   (Knicks, 10)
7) Fred Brown
   (Sonics, 11)
8) Larry Costello
   (Nats-Warriors, 12)

9) Dave Cowens
    (Celtics, 10)
10) Bob Davies
    (Royals, 10)
11) Hal Greer
    (Nats-Warriors, 15)
12) John Havlicek
    (Celtics, 16)
13) Sam Jones
    (Celtics, 12)
14) Willis Reed
    (Knicks, 10)
15) Bill Russell
    (Celtics, 13)
16) Tom Sanders
    (Celtics, 13)
17) Dolph Schayes
    (Nats-Warriors, 16)
18) Jack Twyman
    (Royals, 11)
19) Bobby Wanzer
    (Royals, 10)
20) Jerry West
    (Lakers, 14)

130. Double-Digit Years

1) Paul Arizin (10)
2) Al Attles (11)
3) Bill Bradley (10)
4) Dave Cowens (10)
5) Bob Davies (10)
6) Wayne Embry (11)
7) Bob Ferry (10)
8) Harry Gallatin (10)
9) Tom Gola (10)
10) Happy Hairston (11)
11) Buddy Jeannette (10)
12) Wali Jones (11)
13) Butch Komives (10)
14) Rudy LaRusso (10)
15) Earl Lloyd (10)
16) Ed Macauley (10)
17) Dick McGuire (11)
18) Don Ohl (10)
19) Andy Phillip (11)
20) Willis Reed (10)
21) Gene Shue (10)
22) Jerry Sloan (11)
23) Bobby Wanzer (10)
24) Norm Van Lier (10)
25) Bingo Smith (11)

131. New York Area Schools

1) Seton Hall
2) Columbia
3) Seton Hall
4) St. John's
5) Seton Hall
6) Seton Hall
7) St. John's
8) St. John's
9) LIU
10) NYU
11) NYU
12) St. John's

13) St. John's
14) NYU
15) Seton Hall
16) Seton Hall
17) St. John's
18) St. John's
19) NYU
20) St. John's
21) Columbia
22) Princeton
23) Princeton
24) NYU
25) LIU
26) Seton Hall

27) NYU
28) Seton Hall
29) St. John's
30) NYU
31) NYU
32) LIU
33) Princeton
34) Seton Hall
35) St. John's
36) St. John's
37) Princeton
38) Princeton
39) St. John's
40) Seton Hall

132. The Olympians of Their Times

NCAA Champs

1) Tom Abernethy (1976)
2) Kent Benson (1976)
3) Henry Bibby (1970–72)
4) Quinn Buckner (1976)
5) Tom Burleson (1974)
6) Ralph Drollinger (1973, 1975)
7) Darrell Griffith (1980)
8) Magic Johnson (1979)
9) Marques Johnson (1975)
10) Greg Kelser (1979)
11) Kyle Macy (1978)
12) Scott May (1976)

Olympic Champs

1) Jim Brewer (1972)
2) Michael Brooks (1980)
3) Quinn Buckner (1976)
4) Tom Burleson (1972)
5) Adrian Dantley (1976)
6) Phil Ford (1976)
7) Bill Hanzlik (1980)
8) Tom Henderson (1972)
9) Phil Hubbard (1980)
10) Dwight Jones (1972)
11) Bobby Jones (1972)
12) Mitch Kupchak (1976)
13) Tom Lagarde (1976)

NCAA Champs

13) Andre McCarter
    (1975)
14) Swen Nater
    (1972–73)
15) Rick Robey (1978)
16) David Thompson
    (1974)
17) Richard L. Washington
    (1975)

Olympic Champs

14) Tom McMillen
    (1972)
15) Jo Jo White (1968)

133. Basketball Arenas

1) d	7) v	13) h	19) m
2) b	8) k	14) r	20) p
3) i	9) f	15) n	21) a
4) q	10) o	16) j	22) e
5) w	11) s	17) l	23) c
6) t	12) g	18) u	

134. Seating Space

1) Under (15,700)	13) Under (11,052)
2) Under (15,320)	14) Over (20,149)
3) Over (17,374)	15) Over (19,591)
4) Over (19,548)	16) Over (18,276)
5) Over (17,694)	17) Under (12,666)
6) Over (17,251)	18) Under (12,666)
7) Over (22,366)	19) Under (15,694)
8) Under (13,237)	20) Under (13,841)
9) Under (15,676)	21) Over (40,192)
10) Over (17,092)	22) Under (12,143)
11) Under (16,642)	23) Over (19,035)
12) Over (17,505)	

135. Fathers and Sons

1) Matt, Jr.
2) Dan

3) Jim, Jr.
4) Jan

136. Brother Combos

1) King
2) Jones
3) Williams
4) Wilkes
5) McGuire

6) Mikan
7) Otten
8) Stith
9) Van Arsdale

137. Foreign Talent

1) b
2) e
3) d

4) f
5) a
6) c

138. West of Europe

1) W	6) E	11) W	16) W
2) E	7) E	12) W	17) E
3) E	8) E	13) W	18) W
4) W	9) W	14) E	19) E
5) W	10) E	15) E	20) E

139. Coaches of the Year

1) Red Auerbach
2) Tom Heinsohn
3) Bill Fitch
4) Harry Gallatin
5) Richie Guerin

6) John Kerr
7) Dick Motta
8) Alex Hannum
9) Dolph Schayes
10) Gene Shue

11) Red Holzman	16) Tom Nissalke
12) Bill Sharman	17) Hubie Brown
13) Ray Scott	18) Cotton Fitzsimmons
14) Phil Johnson	19) Jack McKinney
15) Bill Fitch	

140. Winning(?) Coaches

1) W	14) W	27) W	40) W
2) W	15) L	28) W	41) W
3) W	16) W	29) L	42) W
4) W	17) W	30) W	43) W
5) L	18) L	31) W	44) W
6) L	19) W	32) W	45) L
7) W	20) L	33) L	46) L
8) L	21) L	34) W	47) L
9) L	22) W	35) W	48) W
10) L	23) W	36) W	49) W
11) L	24) L	37) W	50) W
12) W	25) W	38) W	
13) L	26) W	39) W	

141. Coaching Championships

Multiple Champs	*One-Time Champs*
1) Red Auerbach	1) Les Harrison
2) John Kundla	2) Dick Motta
3) Alex Hannum*	3) Eddie Gottlieb
4) Bob Leonard**	4) Buddy Jeannette
5) Bill Russell	5) Jack Ramsay
6) Red Holzman	6) Al Cervi
7) Bill Sharman*	7) Al Attles
8) Tom Heinsohn	8) George Senesky
9) Kevin Loughery**	9) Larry Costello

1) Red Auerbach
2) Bill Russell
3) Bob Leonard
4) Kevin Loughery

5) John Kundla
6) Alex Hannum
7) Bill Sharman
8) Buddy Jeannette

* ABA, also.
** ABA, only.

142. Knick Head Coaches

1) Neil Cohalan
2) Joe Lapchick
3) Vince Boryla
4) Fuzzy Levane
5) Carl Braun

6) Eddie Donovan
7) Harry Gallatin
8) Dick McGuire
9) Red Holzman
10) Willis Reed

143. Celtic Head Coaches

1) Honey Russell
2) Doggie Julian
3) Red Auerbach
4) Bill Russell

5) Tom Heinsohn
6) Tom Sanders
7) Dave Cowens
8) Bill Fitch

144. Laker Head Coaches

1) John Kundla
2) George Mikan
3) John Castellani
4) Jim Pollard
5) Fred Schaus
6) Butch van Breda Kolff

7) Joe Mullaney
8) Bill Sharman
9) Jerry West
10) Jack McKinney
11) Paul Westhead
12) Pat Riley

145. Warrior Head Coaches

1) Eddie Gottlieb
2) George Senesky
3) Al Cervi
4) Neil Johnston
5) Frank McGuire
6) Bob Feerick
7) Alex Hannum
8) Bill Sharman
9) George Lee
10) Al Attles
11) John Bach

146. Nat-76er Head Coaches

1) Al Cervi
2) Paul Seymour
3) Alex Hannum
4) Dolph Schayes
5) Jack Ramsay
6) Roy Rubin
7) Kevin Loughery
8) Gene Shue
9) Billy Cunningham

147. Original Coaches: I

1) c
2) i
3) j
4) b
5) d
6) h
7) f
8) m
9) a
10) g
11) e
12) l
13) k

148. Original Coaches: II

1) g
2) b
3) d
4) a
5) k
6) f
7) m
8) e
9) l
10) j
11) c
12) h
13) i

149. Original Coaches: III

1) c
2) k
3) i
4) l
5) j
6) m
7) a
8) e
9) h
10) f
11) g
12) d
13) b

150. Original Coaches: IV

1) e	5) c	9) l	13) b
2) g	6) h	10) m	
3) f	7) a	11) j	
4) d	8) i	12) k	

151. Original Coaches: V

1) d	5) j	9) b
2) g	6) h	10) f
3) k	7) a	11) i
4) c	8) l	12) e

152. Original Coaches: VI

1) j	5) b or d	9) c and g
2) e	6) i	10) c and g
3) h	7) f	11) l
4) b or d	8) k	12) a

153. 60-Win Seasons

1) Red Auerbach	8) Larry Costello
2) Bill Russell	9) Don Nelson
3) Tom Heinsohn	10) Red Holzman
4) Bill Fitch	11) Alex Hannum
5) Larry Brown	12) Billy Cunningham
6) Joe Mullaney	13) La Dell Anderson
7) Bill Sharman	14) K.C. Jones

154. Once Is Enough

1) Bill Russell
2) Joe Mullaney
3) Don Nelson
4) Red Holzman
5) Billy Cunningham
6) La Dell Anderson
7) K.C. Jones

155. Once Is Not Enough

1) Red Auerbach
2) Tom Heinsohn
3) Bill Fitch
4) Larry Brown
5) Bill Sharman

156. Twice Is Not Enough

1) Larry Costello
2) Alex Hannum

157. Coach's Who's Who

1) Bill Sharman
(1971–72 Lakers)
2) Alex Hannum
(1966–67 76ers)
3) Alex Hannum
(1966–67, 1967–68
76ers and 1968–69
Oaks)
4) Bill Fitch (Celtics)
5) Don Nelson (Bucks)
6) Red Auerbach
(Celtics)
7) Bill Russell
(1967–68 and
1968–69 Celtics)
8) Tom Heinsohn
(Celtics)
9) Tom Heinsohn
(1972–73)
10) Joe Mullaney
11) Larry Brown
(1974–75 and
1975–76)
12) Bill Sharman
(1971–72, 1972–73
Lakers and 1970–71
Stars)
13) Larry Costello
(1970–71, 1971–72,
and 1972–73 Bucks)
14) Billy Cunningham
15) Red Holzman
(Knicks)
16) LaDell Anderson
(1971–72)
17) K.C. Jones

158. 50-Win Seasons

Two Times

1) Fred Schaus
2) Butch van Breda Kolff
3) Paul Westhead
4) Jack Ramsay
5) Len Wilkens

Three Times

1) Al Attles
2) Bob Leonard
3) Kevin Loughery
4) John MacLeod

Four Times

1) Gene Shue

Five Times

1) Dick Motta

159. Great Games

1) Wilt Chamberlain
2) David Thompson
3) Elgin Baylor
4) Pete Maravich
5) Rick Barry
6) Joe Fulks (6–8 may be in any order.)
7) Jerry West
8) George Gervin
9) George Mikan

Flash Followup

10) Wilt Chamberlain

160. Championship Sweeps

1) Boston over Minneapolis in 1959
2) Milwaukee over Baltimore in 1971
3) Golden State over Washington in 1975

161. Rookies of the Year

1) Bob McAdoo
2) Ernie Di Gregorio
3) Keith Wilkes
4) Alvan Adams
5) Adrian Dantley
6) Walter Davis
7) Phil Ford
8) Larry Bird
9) Darrell Griffith
10) Buck Williams

162. 1982 College Draft

1) c
2) g
3) n
4) j
5) r
6) v
7) u
8) d
9) k
10) w
11) t
12) s
13) a
14) e
15) o
16) m
17) i
18) b
19) p
20) f
21) q
22) l
23) h

163. 1981-82 Stat Leaders

1) George Gervin
2) Artis Gilmore
3) Moses Malone
4) Kyle Macy
5) George Johnson
6) Johnny Moore
7) Magic Johnson
8) Campy Russell

164. Men at the Mike

1) c
2) f
3) h
4) g
5) a
6) i
7) b
8) e
9) d

THE SCOREBOARD

Record the number of questions that were answered correctly in each quarter.

First Quarter   _____
Second Quarter   _____
Third Quarter   _____
Fourth Quarter   _____
Total   _____

Subtract the total of correct answers from 3333, the number of questions in the game. Then place your score in the left-hand column below and the book's score in the right-hand column.

You _____ The NBA _____

Record the number of games that you won in each quarter.

First Quarter   _____
Second Quarter   _____
Third Quarter   _____
Fourth Quarter   _____
Total   _____

Subtract the total of games won from 164, the number of quizzes in the game. Then place your score in the left-hand column below and the books score in the right-hand column.

You _____ The NBA _____

Place the number of wins over the number of games played. Divide the bottom number into the top number, and you have your winning percentage. Now compare it with the winning percentages of every NBA champion listed below.

How did you do? Congratulations. Good game!

WINNING PERCENTAGES

.841 Los Angeles
    (1971–72)
.840 Philadelphia
    (1966–67)
.805 Milwaukee (1970–71)
.787 Boston (1959–60)
.756 Boston (1980–81)
.750 Minneapolis
    (1949–50)
.750 Boston (1961–62)
.738 Boston (1961–62)
.733 Minneapolis
    (1948–49)
.732 New York (1969–70)
.732 Los Angeles
    (1979–80)
.725 Boston (1962–63)
.722 Boston (1958–59)
.722 Boston (1960–61)
.715 Boston (1964–65)
.695 New York (1972–73)
.686 Minneapolis
    (1952–53)

.675 Boston (1965–66)
.659 Boston (1967–68)
.659 Boston (1975–76)
.639 Minneapolis
    (1953–54)
.634 Seattle (1978–79)
.625 Philadelphia
    (1955–56)
.611 Boston (1956–57)
.606 Minneapolis
    (1951–52)
.603 Rochester (1950–51)
.598 Portland (1976–77)
.597 Syracuse (1954–55)
.585 Boston (1968–69)
.585 Golden State
    (1974–75)
.583 Philadelphia
    (1946–47)
.583 Baltimore (1947–48)
.569 St. Louis (1957–58)
.537 Washington
    (1977–78)

DOM FORKER was born the day Joe DiMaggio hit three for six in the fifth game of DiMaggio's first World Series. A coach and former college pitcher, the author teaches English and journalism in Frenchtown, New Jersey. He lives with his wife and three sons in Milford, New Jersey. He is the author of ALMOST EVERYTHING YOU'VE EVER WANTED TO KNOW ABOUT BASEBALL, THE ULTIMATE BASEBALL QUIZ BOOK, THE ULTIMATE YANKEE BASEBALL QUIZ BOOK, and THE ULTIMATE WORLD SERIES QUIZ BOOK.